The Gentleman's Dominion
A Foundational Guide to Professional and Social Etiquette

Copyright © 2025, Daniel Pavia
All rights reserved.

First published 2025 by Sovereign House Publishing Pty Ltd

This publication is protected by international copyright laws. No part of this book may be reproduced, stored in a retrieval system, or transmitted in any form or by any means, including electronic, digital, mechanical, photocopying, recording, scanning, or otherwise, without the prior written permission of the publisher, except in the case of brief quotations embodied in critical articles and reviews.

For permissions and licensing enquiries, contact:
info@sovereignhousepublishing.com

ISBN 978-1-7641499-0-7

Editor: Kym Dunbar

Printed in the United States of America and Australia

Contents

Disclaimer	vi
Dedication	viii
1 Introduction	1
2 Chapter 1	3
The Modern Gentleman – Defining Values and Principles	3
Redefining Gentlemanly Conduct in the 21st Century	3
Confidence, Humility and Resilience	6
The Importance of Self-awareness and Personal Growth	8
Respect and Consideration	10
A Harmonious Approach	14
3 Chapter 2	17
Mastering the Art of Conversation	17
The Cornerstone of Engaging Dialogue	17
Expressing Yourself with Clarity and Grace	20
Engaging Others through Narrative	23
Diplomacy and Tact	27
Establishing Meaningful Connections	30
4 Chapter 3	34
Business Etiquette – Protocol and Professionalism	34
Making a Positive First Impression in Business	34
Building Relationships in Professional Settings	37
Punctuality and Professional Demeanor	41
Maintaining Professional Standards	44
Impressing Clients and Colleagues	48
5 Chapter 4	52
Social Etiquette – Grace and Refinement	52

Making a Strong First Impression in Social Settings	52
Mastering Table Manners and Social Graces	56
Creating a Welcoming and Memorable Experience	61
Thoughtfulness and Consideration	65
Engaging with Diverse Groups	69
6 Chapter 5	73
Personal Style – Cultivating a Refined Image	73
Timeless Elegance	73
Enhancing your Appearance	76
Adding Personality and Refinement	79
Maintaining a Polished Look	83
Adapting your Style	86
7 Chapter 6	90
The Art of Appreciation – Wine, Spirits and Cigars	90
Understanding the Basics	90
Classic Drinks and Modern Mixology	94
A Gentleman's Pursuit	97
Moderation and Awareness	100
Enhancing Culinary Experiences	103
8 Chapter 7	107
Travel Etiquette – Navigating Global Settings	107
Customs and Cultural Nuances	107
Efficiency and Respect	110
Professionalism and Courtesy	112
Adapting to Cultural Differences	115
Public Transit and Private Vehicles	118
Etiquette in Hired Cars and Private Transport	118
Cultural Sensitivities in Transportation	119
The Broader Perspective	120
9 Chapter 8	121
Digital Decorum – Navigating the Online World	121
Crafting a Professional Image	121
Professionalism in Digital Communication	124

Engaging Respectfully and Appropriately	128
Protecting your Digital Footprint	131
Modern Etiquette in the Digital Age	134
The Golden Rule Reimagined for the Digital Age	134
Common Mistakes in the Digital Era	135
Passive Aggression and Subtweeting	135
Ghosting in Professional Environments	136
Oversharing on Personal and Professional Platforms	136
Lengthy Audio Messages or Unsolicited Voice Notes	137
Digital Character as Digital Presence	137
10 Chapter 9	**139**
Building Meaningful Relationships – Connection and Legacy	139
Cultivating Meaningful Bonds	139
Communication and Respect	142
Nurturing Bonds across Generations	145
The Power of Open and Honest Communication	145
Consistent Engagement: Small Gestures Matter	146
Embracing Generational Differences	146
Addressing and Healing Family Conflicts	147
Providing Practical and Emotional Support	147
Adapting to Change and Embracing Growth	148
Guiding and Supporting Others	148
Contributing to Society	152
References	156
Acknowledgements	159
Author Biography	161

Disclaimer

This book is intended for informational and educational purposes only. The author is not a licensed medical, financial, legal, or investment professional, and the contents herein do not constitute professional advice. Readers are advised to consult with qualified professionals before acting on any information provided.

The author and publisher make no representations or warranties regarding the accuracy, applicability, suitability, or completeness of the information contained in this publication. Any reliance on the material is strictly at the reader's own risk.

The discussion of alcohol, cigars, and nicotine products is for cultural and informational purposes only. The author does not endorse or encourage the use of these substances—especially by underage readers or in violation of local laws. Any use should be compliant with applicable laws and undertaken at the reader's discretion and risk.

Nothing in this publication creates a professional-client relationship between the reader and the author or publisher.

Some insights and inspiration throughout this book were drawn from articles, essays, and thought leadership pieces across a variety of online platforms and publications. Full credit is provided in the References section. All effort has been made to reinterpret these ideas in an original and transformative way aligned with the author's unique perspective and voice.

The reader agrees to indemnify and hold harmless the author, publisher, and their respective affiliates, officers, directors, employees, agents, and representatives from any and all claims, demands, losses, liabilities, damages, or expenses (including reasonable legal fees) arising out of or in connection with personal injury, property damage, or third-party claims resulting from the use or misuse of the information provided.

To the fullest extent permitted by law, the author and publisher disclaim all liability for any direct, indirect, incidental, or consequential damages arising from reliance on this publication. In jurisdictions where such limitations are not enforceable, liability is limited to the maximum extent permitted by law.

This disclaimer and indemnity clause are governed solely by the laws of Australia. Any disputes arising out of the use of this publication shall be subject to the exclusive jurisdiction of the Australian courts, except where mandatory consumer protection laws in the reader's country require otherwise.

By reading this book, you acknowledge that you are fully responsible for your decisions and actions and agree to the terms set forth above.

Dedication

To the enduring ideals of gentlemanly conduct and the men courageous enough to embody them in a constantly evolving world, this book is for you. It speaks to those who aspire to lead lives of purpose, integrity, and influence, balancing the grace of tradition with the boldness of innovation.

This book is dedicated to those who value respect, consideration, and mindful engagement as the foundations of meaningful relationships and a life of substance. To the ones who challenge outdated norms, defy societal expectations, and redefine what it means to be a gentleman in the 21st century, you are the architects of modern elegance.

Let this book be your compass, guiding you in refining not only your style but also your character. Being a gentleman isn't about achieving perfection; it's about embracing progression, being a journey of continuous growth, self-improvement, and a commitment to leaving the world better than you found it.

This is an invitation, a starting point, and a celebration of the courage it takes to live with purpose, humility, and unwavering dedication. Here's to the journey ahead.

Introduction

This book serves as a definitive guide for navigating the complexities of modern life as a gentleman of distinction and character. Designed for men of all ages and backgrounds, it offers timeless principles and practical guidance for those who aspire to personal growth, professional success, and the confidence to excel in any setting.

The concept of a gentleman has evolved, transcending outdated stereotypes to reflect a refined, inclusive identity. Today's gentleman embodies a harmonious blend of enduring values, such as integrity, respect, and humility, with the demands and sensibilities of the contemporary world. This book explores the essence of gentlemanly conduct, offering insights into etiquette for both social and professional contexts, strategies for personal development and the cultivation of meaningful relationships.

This work goes beyond superficial advice, focusing on building resilience, self-awareness, and mindfulness, which are essential qualities for navigating life's challenges. Whether managing high-pressure meetings, leaving a lasting impression at social events, or fostering deep personal connections, this book equips readers with the tools to handle every situation with poise and elegance.

Within these pages, readers will find practical guidance on mastering the art of conversation, curating a versatile wardrobe, appreciating fine wines and cigars, and navigating the digital world with professionalism and grace. Far more than a style guide, this book serves as a comprehensive roadmap for leading a purposeful and impactful life.

The goal is not to impose a rigid standard of behavior but to empower individuals to cultivate their unique style, rooted in respect, integrity, and an enduring commitment to self-improvement. This book invites readers to embark on a lifelong journey of refinement, self-discovery, and the pursuit of excellence in every aspect of life.

Chapter 1

The Modern Gentleman – Defining Values and Principles

Redefining Gentlemanly Conduct in the 21st Century

The concept of the "gentleman" has transformed significantly throughout history. What defined gentlemanly conduct in the Victorian era, rooted in rigid social hierarchies and prescribed behaviors, differs dramatically from the expectations placed on men in the 21st century. Outdated stereotypes often depict the gentleman as aloof, emotionally reserved, and confined to the realm of period dramas or historical fiction. This perception is not only inaccurate but diminishes the evolving ideals of modern gentlemanly conduct. At its core, the essence of being a gentleman remains unchanged: respect, integrity, and consideration for others are timeless principles. However, their expression must adapt to the realities of today. The modern gentleman is not defined by adherence to archaic rules but by his ability to navigate contemporary challenges with grace, empathy, and a strong moral compass. He embraces both tradition and progress, challenges outdated norms, and commits to personal growth and self-awareness.

A key shift lies in the understanding of masculinity. The traditional image of a stoic, emotionless gentleman is giving way to a more empathetic and holistic approach. The modern gentleman values emotional intelligence, expressing feelings in healthy ways. This maturity fosters stronger, more authentic relationships and enhances his resilience. Open communication, active listening, and empathy are hallmarks of his character. He understands that vulnerability is not a weakness but a strength that enables deeper connections and personal growth. The modern gentleman rejects notions of entitlement and superiority. He champions equality, respecting the dignity of all individuals regardless of gender, race, ethnicity, sexuality, or socioeconomic background. He actively opposes prejudice and discrimination, advocating for justice and fairness in all areas of life. Recognizing historical injustices, he works toward building a more equitable society. For him, true strength lies in respect, inclusion, and collaboration, not dominance.

In a world increasingly shaped by technology, the modern gentleman understands the importance of digital decorum. He uses online platforms responsibly, maintaining a professional and respectful presence. By avoiding impulsive or insensitive comments, he ensures his digital footprint aligns with his values. Technology becomes a tool for fostering meaningful connections, not a distraction from genuine human interaction.

Personal responsibility now includes environmental consciousness and ethical consumerism. The modern gentleman considers the impact of his actions on the environment, striving to make choices that support sustainability. Whether through reducing waste, supporting ethical businesses, or minimizing his ecological footprint, he recognizes that his actions contribute to a healthier planet. While personal style remains a hallmark of gentlemanly conduct, it has evolved beyond rigid fashion norms. The modern gentleman curates a wardrobe that reflects his individuality, blending timeless elegance with contemporary flair. He values quality craftsmanship and embraces versatility, ensuring his style serves as an authentic expression of his personality and values.

CHAPTER 1

The journey of the modern gentleman is defined by continuous self-reflection and growth. He prioritizes lifelong learning, developing skills and knowledge that enhance his personal and professional life. From physical wellness and emotional intelligence to financial literacy and ethical conduct, he strives to expand his horizons and refine his character. He learns from mistakes, addresses biases, and seeks to improve continuously. Genuine connections are central to a fulfilling life. The modern gentleman nurtures relationships built on mutual respect, trust, and open communication. He listens actively, empathizes with others' perspectives, and provides support when needed. Recognizing the value of strong relationships, he invests in cultivating them with family, friends, and colleagues alike.

The modern gentleman is committed to making a positive impact on society. Whether through mentoring, volunteering, or advocating for social justice, he uses his influence to uplift others and contribute to a better future. His dedication to social responsibility reflects his understanding of humanity's interconnectedness and his desire to leave a meaningful legacy. The 21st-century gentleman is an evolving archetype, blending timeless virtues with the demands of a changing world. Guided by respect, integrity, and compassion, he navigates life with a balance of strength and sensitivity. His conduct is not bound by rigid rules but reflects dynamic values that shape his character and actions.

Becoming a modern gentleman is a journey of continuous refinement, self-awareness, and adaptability. It's about striving for excellence, not perfection but embracing tradition while boldly forging a path forward. The true mark of a gentleman lies in his ability to lead with integrity, inspire through action, and contribute meaningfully to the world around him.

Confidence, Humility and Resilience

The foundation upon which a modern gentleman builds his character rests on three core values: confidence, humility, and resilience. These are not merely abstract ideals but actively cultivated attributes that shape his interactions, decisions, and, ultimately, his legacy. Confidence, however, is not about arrogance or self-aggrandizement. It's a quiet assurance born of self-awareness, competence, and a genuine belief in one's capabilities. It allows a man to navigate challenges with grace and composure, articulate his opinions respectfully, and stand firm in his convictions without resorting to aggression or intimidation.

Cultivating confidence begins with self-reflection. Recognizing strengths and weaknesses with honesty is crucial. Still, it's not about pursuing unattainable perfection but identifying potential and taking deliberate steps toward realizing it. This may involve seeking mentorship, pursuing further education, or dedicating time to mastering a specific skill. Continuous learning itself fosters confidence, demonstrating a commitment to self-improvement and a readiness to embrace challenges. Confidence also stems from competence, encompassing not just technical proficiency but also emotional intelligence; the ability to understand and regulate one's emotions while empathizing with others.[1] A man who is confident in both his abilities and emotional intelligence can navigate complex social situations with tact, manage stress effectively, and strengthen his relationships.

Equally important is humility. Humility is not self-deprecation but an awareness of one's limitations, a willingness to acknowledge mistakes, and an appreciation for the contributions of others. A humble gentleman admits when he is wrong and seeks opportunities to learn and grow from those experiences. He understands that success is often a collaborative effort and avoids claiming undue credit, appreciating the value others bring regardless of their social standing or professional achievements. Humility fosters genuine respect for others, encouraging meaningful connections based on

CHAPTER 1

mutual trust.

Active listening is a key practice of humility. It goes beyond simply hearing words to engaging with the speaker's message, asking thoughtful questions, and responding with genuine interest. By truly listening, a man demonstrates respect and creates an environment where others feel valued. Humility also includes acknowledging the support of others, recognizing that individual accomplishments often rest on the encouragement and efforts of mentors, teammates, or loved ones. Mistakes, too, are viewed as opportunities for growth rather than weaknesses to conceal. A man's willingness to learn from setbacks exemplifies his commitment to personal development.

Resilience, the third cornerstone, is the ability to recover from setbacks, persevere through adversity, and grow stronger in the process. Challenges, whether personal losses, professional disappointments, or unforeseen difficulties, are inevitable, but the modern gentleman adapts to these circumstances with determination and grace. Resilience is not just about enduring hardship but about proactively seeking solutions, analyzing challenges, and implementing strategies to move forward.

Developing resilience involves building a strong support network of positive and supportive individuals who offer encouragement, guidance, and perspective during difficult times. Seeking help when needed is not a sign of weakness but of wisdom and strength. Resilience also requires adaptability. Life's challenges evolve, and the ability to adjust strategies and approaches accordingly ensures continued growth and effectiveness.

Confidence, humility, and resilience are deeply interconnected. Confidence rooted in humility fosters respectful and genuine interactions. Humility enhances resilience by cultivating openness to learning and growth from setbacks. Resilience, in turn, strengthens confidence in one's ability to face life's challenges. Together, these values form the foundation of a modern gentleman's character, guiding him to navigate life with integrity, purpose, and grace.

Cultivating these core values is an ongoing process, a lifelong journey of self-reflection and refinement. It's not about achieving a static state of perfection but embracing continuous growth and evolution. The modern gentleman strives to embody these principles not only in his personal endeavors but also in his interactions with others and his contributions to society. This pursuit defines the modern gentleman, not as a relic of the past but as a forward-thinking individual who embodies timeless virtues in a dynamic and complex world.

The journey to becoming a modern gentleman is a testament to the enduring power of these foundational values. Confidence, humility, and resilience shape not just the individual but also the world he influences, creating a life of purpose, fulfillment, and distinction.

The Importance of Self-awareness and Personal Growth

The journey to becoming a modern gentleman is not a destination but a continuous process of refinement. While confidence, humility, and resilience provide a strong foundation, their true power lies in their application through self-awareness and personal growth. This requires deep introspection, a willingness to confront shortcomings, and a commitment to lifelong learning. It's about objectively assessing your strengths and actively working to enhance them. Genuine confidence is not boastful but grounded in a realistic understanding of self.

Mindfulness plays a crucial role in this process. It's more than meditation; it's about cultivating present-moment awareness, paying attention to thoughts, emotions, and actions without judgment. This heightened awareness helps identify behavioral patterns, both positive and negative, that shape character. Do you struggle with patience, active listening, or dominating conversations? Mindful observation is the first step in addressing these tendencies. Keeping a journal, for instance, can help track progress, recognize recurring patterns, and foster deeper self-awareness. Honest self-assessment is not about self-criticism but is about evaluating strengths and weaknesses objectively. It requires vulnerability, such as the willingness to acknowledge where improvement is needed.

Self-awareness extends beyond personal attributes to interactions with others. How do you respond in challenging situations? Do you react defensively or with calm consideration? Do you seek to understand differing perspectives or rigidly cling to your own? These reflections provide valuable insights, allowing for conscious choices that lead to meaningful growth.

Personal improvement is rarely linear. Setbacks and frustrations are inevitable, making resilience essential. The ability to learn from mistakes and maintain a positive outlook transforms obstacles into opportunities. Every misstep becomes a lesson, shifting the focus from self-criticism to growth. Cultivating emotional intelligence is key to building resilience. Understanding and managing emotions while recognizing those of others fosters empathy, as an essential skill for navigating complex social interactions. Reading emotional cues, responding with sensitivity, and strengthening relationships all contribute to the refinement of character.

Growth also involves expanding knowledge and skills beyond traditional education. A modern gentleman embraces lifelong learning, whether through acquiring new hobbies, mastering a language, or engaging in thoughtful conversations with diverse individuals. Each experience broadens perspective and enhances adaptability. In a rapidly evolving world shaped by technological advancements and globalization, continuous learning ensures relevance and effectiveness in all aspects of life.

Seeking mentorship is another invaluable step. A trusted mentor, whether a friend, family member, or professional can provide guidance, perspective, and support. Learning from others extends beyond formal mentorship; being open to constructive criticism and actively seeking feedback accelerates personal development.

A commitment to self-improvement extends to financial literacy and health. Understanding budgeting, investing, and financial planning fosters security and stability. Likewise, prioritizing physical and mental well-being is integral. Regular exercise, a balanced diet, and sufficient rest enhance overall quality of life, while mindfulness, time in nature, and engaging in fulfilling activities support mental health. These aren't indulgences but investments in long-term well-being.

Beyond personal development, a modern gentleman cultivates a sense of purpose by contributing to something greater than himself. Volunteering, mentoring, or engaging in acts of generosity enriches not only others' lives but also his own. This broader perspective reinforces humility and resilience, demonstrating a genuine commitment to making a difference. True personal growth becomes a journey of shared progress and collaborative betterment.

Ultimately, the path to becoming a modern gentleman is a lifelong pursuit of self-awareness, refinement, and purpose. It's about developing confidence rooted in humility, resilience strengthened through mindfulness, and an unwavering dedication to personal growth. The measure of a gentleman lies not in outward appearances but in the integrity of his character, the depth of his empathy, and the impact he makes. This journey is one of constant reflection and adaptation; an ongoing pursuit of becoming the best version of oneself.

Respect and Consideration

Etiquette, at its core, is about respect and consideration. It's not a rigid set of rules meant to stifle individuality but a framework for navigating social and professional interactions with grace and thoughtfulness. In today's fast-paced world, where communication often feels transactional and impersonal,

CHAPTER 1

the ability to demonstrate genuine respect is a rare and valuable asset. It sets you apart and leaves a lasting positive impression. More than simple politeness, etiquette is about actively fostering a positive environment for everyone involved.

Consider the power of a simple "please" and "thank you". These seemingly minor phrases form the foundation of respectful communication. They acknowledge the effort and time of others, signifying appreciation for their contributions, no matter how small. Similarly, a sincere apology, when warranted, demonstrates humility and a willingness to take responsibility for one's actions. It fosters trust and repairs damaged relationships. The absence of these gestures can create distance and resentment, hindering meaningful connections.

Respect and consideration extend beyond verbal communication. Punctuality, for instance, is a profound expression of respect for another person's time. Arriving late to a meeting, dinner, or social engagement sends a message that your time is more valuable than theirs. It disrupts the flow of events and demonstrates a lack of consideration. Conversely, arriving on time, or even slightly early, shows professionalism and allows for a more relaxed and productive start, setting a positive tone for the interaction.

Active listening is another crucial element of respectful engagement. In today's distraction-filled world, the ability to truly listen without interrupting or preemptively formulating a response, is a rare and highly valued skill. It shows genuine interest in another person's thoughts and feelings, creating a connection based on mutual understanding and empathy. Asking open-ended questions, encouraging elaboration, and actively engaging in conversation fosters authentic dialogue and strengthens relationships, both personally and professionally.

Beyond individual interactions, etiquette plays a critical role in fostering a positive and collaborative work environment. Respecting colleagues' opinions, even when you disagree, acknowledging contributions, and maintaining professional boundaries are essential for a harmonious and productive workplace. This respect extends to all levels, from interns to senior executives. A culture of mutual respect builds trust, enhances teamwork, and ultimately leads to greater success.

The impact of etiquette extends far beyond immediate interactions. It shapes your reputation, influencing how people perceive you and how they choose to engage with you in the future. A reputation for being respectful, considerate, and well-mannered can open doors to opportunities that might otherwise remain closed. Conversely, a reputation for rudeness or inconsideration can significantly hinder personal and professional growth.

The digital age presents unique challenges to maintaining good etiquette. The anonymity of online interactions can sometimes encourage less considerate behavior, but the principles of respect and thoughtfulness remain paramount. Think before you post, avoid inflammatory language, and be mindful of the impact your words can have on others. Responding thoughtfully and professionally to emails and other digital communications shows respect for the recipient's time and demonstrates a high level of professionalism.

Understanding and practicing appropriate table manners is another key aspect of etiquette in both business and social settings. While formal dinners may require a more intricate knowledge of etiquette, even informal settings benefit from basic table manners. Knowing how to use cutlery properly, engaging in thoughtful conversation, and conducting oneself with grace reflects positively on your character and conveys respect for your host and fellow diners. These small yet significant actions display consideration and a level of sophistication that enhances any situation.

Proper phone etiquette is another frequently overlooked yet crucial aspect of modern interactions. Avoid answering calls during important meetings or conversations, and always excuse yourself gracefully when necessary.

CHAPTER 1

When initiating calls, state your name and purpose clearly. Respecting the other person's time and minimizing unnecessary interruptions demonstrate professionalism and thoughtfulness.

Beyond these specific behaviors, the foundation of all good etiquette lies in empathy and emotional intelligence. Putting yourself in another person's shoes, understanding their perspective, and responding with sensitivity and compassion are crucial for navigating complex social situations. This requires self-awareness, recognizing how your actions and words might impact others and adjusting your behavior accordingly. It's a skill honed over time through experience and introspection.

Consider the impact of body language. Maintaining eye contact, offering a firm handshake when appropriate, and using proper posture all communicate respect and confidence.[2] Conversely, avoiding eye contact, slouching, or fidgeting can convey disinterest or even disrespect. These nonverbal cues often speak louder than words, shaping how others perceive you both consciously and subconsciously.

Finally, cultivate a genuine interest in other people. Ask about their lives, their work, and their passions, and actively listen to their responses. This demonstrates a level of care and respect that goes beyond mere politeness. It builds stronger relationships and enriches your own life through meaningful connections. Being present, engaged, and genuinely interested in others leaves a lasting positive impression.

The true mastery of etiquette isn't about memorizing a list of rules; it's about cultivating a mindset of respect and consideration. It's about understanding the impact of your actions and words on those around you and striving to create a positive and harmonious environment. By embodying these principles, you not only enhance your personal and professional interactions but also contribute to a more civilized and respectful society. Good etiquette is a testament to character, reflecting integrity, empathy, and a genuine desire to treat others with kindness and thoughtfulness. It's not about adhering to archaic rules but it's about fostering authentic connections built on mutual respect and understanding. Ultimately, it's a lifelong journey of refinement, an ongoing evolution toward becoming the best version of yourself, more specifically a true modern gentleman.

A Harmonious Approach

The challenge for the modern gentleman is not to reject tradition outright but to discern its enduring wisdom and adapt it to the complexities of the 21st century. The ideals of chivalry, honor, and integrity remain as relevant as ever, yet their expression requires a nuanced understanding of evolving societal expectations. Blind adherence to outdated customs can appear rigid, even anachronistic, while completely rejecting tradition risks losing essential grounding and civility. The key is to find a harmonious balance, a synthesis of timeless principles and contemporary sensibilities.

Consider the art of conversation, a cornerstone of gentlemanly conduct. Traditional etiquette emphasized formal speech, careful diction, and a measured pace. While these qualities remain valuable, demonstrating respect for both the other person and the exchange itself, the modern context demands a more fluid and adaptable approach. The ability to actively listen, engage thoughtfully with diverse viewpoints, and adjust one's communication style to the situation is crucial. This means being comfortable discussing a wide range of topics, from current events and cultural trends to personal experiences and professional aspirations, while maintaining respect and avoiding contentiousness. It's about fostering genuine connection rather than dominating the conversation. The modern gentleman is not just a skilled conversationalist but also a good listener, capable of drawing others out and making them feel heard and valued.

Similarly, sartorial elegance remains pertinent, though with a contemporary twist. A perfectly tailored suit still projects confidence and authority, but

CHAPTER 1

it should never feel constricting or out of place. The modern gentleman understands the importance of dressing appropriately for the occasion, blending classic elements with modern touches to create a style that is both sophisticated and individualistic. He values a well-crafted capsule wardrobe, capable of transitioning seamlessly between formal and informal settings. He might pair a classic blazer with modern chinos and stylish sneakers or opt for a tailored suit in a contemporary cut and fabric. The goal is to present a polished appearance that reflects self-awareness and attention to detail without being overly formal or ostentatious. Quality takes precedence over quantity, with timeless pieces chosen for versatility and refinement.

Punctuality remains an essential element of good manners, as respecting others' time is a fundamental expression of courtesy and consideration. While unforeseen delays can occur, making a genuine effort to be on time for appointments, meetings, and social gatherings demonstrates professionalism and respect. The modern gentleman recognizes that punctuality reflects not only his regard for others but also self-discipline and a commitment to efficiency. He plans accordingly, allows ample travel time, and communicates proactively if delays are unavoidable. This extends beyond simply arriving at the designated time; it encompasses preparedness and organization, ensuring a smooth and efficient start to any engagement.

Navigating digital etiquette presents a unique challenge. The rapid evolution of technology has introduced new complexities in communication and social interaction. Traditional principles of respect, consideration, and courtesy remain just as important in the digital sphere, though their application requires a nuanced understanding of online platforms and communication norms. The modern gentleman is mindful of his digital footprint, maintaining a professional and respectful online presence. He values thoughtful and well-crafted communication, avoiding impulsive or inflammatory statements. He skillfully navigates social media, using it to build professional networks and engage in constructive dialogue while maintaining a balance between personal and professional interactions. Aware of the potential for misunderstandings in online communication, he strives for clarity, conciseness, and consideration in his digital interactions.

Furthermore, generosity extends beyond material gifts. The modern gentleman recognizes the value of giving his time, energy, and expertise to support causes he believes in. He participates in community service, mentors others, and contributes to charitable endeavors, reflecting a commitment to social responsibility and a desire to make a positive impact. True gentlemanliness transcends personal gain, encompassing a broader dedication to societal well-being.

Continuous self-improvement is another defining characteristic. The modern gentleman is a lifelong learner, constantly seeking to expand his knowledge, refine his skills, and develop his character. He engages in intellectual pursuits, reads widely, and embraces new challenges that push him beyond his comfort zone. This commitment is not about self-aggrandizement but about striving for personal excellence. He understands that growth is an ongoing journey requiring effort, discipline, and self-reflection.

Ultimately, balancing tradition and modernity means upholding the core values of gentlemanliness while adapting their expression to contemporary life. It involves recognizing the enduring wisdom of traditional principles while integrating the insights and experiences of a rapidly changing world. The modern gentleman is not a relic clinging to outdated customs but a thoughtful, adaptable individual who embraces both tradition and progress. He strives to live with purpose, integrity, and genuine consideration for others, understanding that true refinement is not merely a matter of appearances but a reflection of character. His journey toward gentlemanliness is lifelong, marked by continuous learning, self-reflection, and a willingness to evolve. The result is a man who is not only well-mannered and stylish but also insightful, empathetic, and deeply engaged with the world around him.

Chapter 2

Mastering the Art of Conversation

The Cornerstone of Engaging Dialogue

Active listening is more than hearing words; it's about genuinely engaging with the speaker and showing a sincere interest in their message. It's the foundation of any meaningful conversation, fostering understanding, building rapport, and strengthening connections. In today's fast-paced world, where distractions are common and multitasking is often prioritized, mastering the skill of active listening requires conscious effort and consistent practice. However, it's an investment that pays significant dividends both personally and professionally.

At the core of active listening is attentiveness. This involves minimizing distractions, setting aside your own thoughts, and focusing entirely on the speaker. Turn off your phone, resist interrupting, and avoid formulating your response while they are speaking. Give them your full attention, create space for them to express themselves without feeling rushed. This attentive posture speaks volumes, showing respect for their message. Visual cues are crucial by maintaining eye contact, nodding occasionally to signal understanding, and using open body language. Avoid crossing your arms or legs, as this can convey disinterest or defensiveness.

Active listening goes beyond simply hearing the words; it's about understanding the speaker's deeper message, including their emotions and intentions. Pay attention to tone of voice, body language, and the broader context. Are they expressing frustration, excitement, or concern? What are the emotions underlying their words? This requires empathy and the ability to step into the speaker's shoes, seeing the situation from their perspective. This empathetic approach is key to building rapport and creating a genuine connection.

To show your understanding, use both verbal and nonverbal cues to acknowledge the speaker's message. Summarizing or paraphrasing what you've heard is an effective way to ensure clarity and demonstrate that you're truly listening. For example, you might say, "So, if I understand correctly, you're saying that…" or "It sounds like you're feeling frustrated because…" These phrases indicate engagement and offer the speaker an opportunity to clarify any misunderstandings. Asking clarifying questions is equally important. Don't interrupt to ask a question; instead, wait for a natural pause. Phrases like "Can you elaborate on that?" or "I'm curious about…" encourage further discussion and show your interest.

Active listening is not a passive process; it's dynamic and requires ongoing engagement. It involves thoughtful responses, both verbal and nonverbal, reflecting your understanding of the speaker's message. Avoid irrelevant comments or abruptly changing the subject. Instead, build on what the speaker has said by adding your own insights and perspectives. Share relevant anecdotes or observations, but keep the focus on the speaker and their message.

Consider the context. In professional settings, active listening is essential for effective communication, conflict resolution, and building strong relationships. By listening attentively to colleagues' concerns and actively seeking their input, you contribute to a collaborative and respectful work environment. In social settings, it's equally important for building meaningful friendships and romantic relationships. Showing genuine interest in others' thoughts and feelings creates a safe space for open communication and deeper connections. Active listening is the foundation of strong, lasting relationships.

Refining your ability to listen actively is a gradual process, shaped by a commitment to self-improvement. It requires self-awareness, empathy, and a real desire to connect with others. Regular practice is key. Make an effort to engage in active listening in different settings, gradually honing your skills. Observe experienced listeners. How do they engage in conversations? What techniques do they use to demonstrate attentiveness? Analyze successful interactions, both in your own life and those you observe, and incorporate those techniques into your communication style.

Reflect on your listening habits. Do you often interrupt? Do you find yourself thinking about your response while someone else is speaking? Are you fully engaged, or does your mind wander? Recognizing your weaknesses is the first step toward improvement. Once you identify areas to work on, you can focus on refining your listening skills, gradually becoming a more effective and engaging conversationalist.

Nonverbal cues also play a major role. These can be even more powerful than words in conveying attentiveness. For example, maintaining eye contact shows engagement and respect. Avoid staring too intensely, which can come off as aggressive or intimidating. Instead, use a natural, relaxed gaze, occasionally shifting your focus without breaking eye contact entirely. Mirroring the speaker's body language subtly (without overdoing it) can also strengthen rapport and create a sense of connection. However, do not mimic every movement, as this may seem insincere or mocking.

The importance of summarizing and paraphrasing cannot be overstated.

These techniques show your understanding and give the speaker a chance to clarify any misunderstandings. Rather than repeating their words verbatim, express their ideas in your own words. This shows you've internalized the meaning and grasped the emotions behind the message. For example, if someone says, "I'm feeling overwhelmed by the workload," you could paraphrase this as, "It sounds like you're stressed and burdened by all the work you have to do." This indicates that you've understood not only the words but the underlying emotion as well.

In conclusion, active listening is a vital skill for building strong relationships, navigating complex situations, and achieving success both personally and professionally. It requires conscious effort, ongoing practice, and a true commitment to understanding others. By mastering this skill, you will forge deeper connections, improve communication, and elevate your interactions to a new level of engagement. Active listening is an investment in yourself and your relationships, offering immeasurable returns. The more you practice, the more natural and instinctive it becomes, transforming your ability to engage in meaningful conversations.

Expressing Yourself with Clarity and Grace

Building on the foundation of active listening, the next key element in mastering conversation is effective communication, such as expressing yourself with clarity and grace. This involves more than just stringing words together; it's about crafting your message with precision, ensuring it resonates with your audience and serves its intended purpose. It requires an understanding of both the spoken and unspoken aspects of communication, including word choice, tone of voice, body language, and an awareness of the social context.

Clear and concise communication is crucial in any interaction, whether it's a casual conversation with a friend or a high-stakes business negotiation. Ambiguity can lead to misunderstandings, misinterpretations, and, ultimately, failed communication. The ability to articulate your thoughts and ideas in a straightforward, easily digestible manner is a valuable skill that sets apart those who excel in both interpersonal relationships and professional settings.

Consider the impact of word choice. A simple change in wording can dramatically alter the meaning and impact of your message. For example, "I suggest" conveys a recommendation, while "I insist" projects a forceful demand. The choice depends entirely on the context and your desired outcome. Similarly, using jargon or overly technical language in a conversation with someone unfamiliar with those terms can create a barrier to understanding and frustrate both parties. Always strive for language that is accessible and suitable for your audience.

Tailoring your language and tone to the situation is equally important. A formal business meeting demands a different approach than a friendly gathering with close friends. In a professional setting, your language should be precise, respectful, and free from slang or colloquialisms. Maintain a formal tone, using appropriate titles and addressing individuals with courtesy. However, in informal settings, a more relaxed style is acceptable, allowing for greater spontaneity and expressiveness. Even so, respect and consideration for others should always be maintained.

The tone of your voice significantly impacts how your message is received. A monotone delivery, no matter how eloquent, can sound dull and disengaging. Varying your pitch and volume emphasizes key points, adds dynamism to keep your audience engaged. Your tone can also convey emotions and intentions that words alone might not capture. A warm, friendly tone fosters connection, while a harsh or condescending tone can alienate and offend. Be mindful of your tone, ensure it complements your message.

Nonverbal communication plays a powerful role in expressing yourself effectively. Your body language, including posture, gestures, facial expressions, and eye contact, often communicates as much, if not more, than words.

Good posture conveys confidence, while slouching suggests disinterest. Measured gestures can enhance your message, while excessive gestures may be distracting or even offensive. Maintaining eye contact shows engagement and respect, whereas avoiding it can signal disinterest or dishonesty. Be mindful that your body language aligns with your spoken words and the context of the conversation.[3]

Understanding cultural nuances is also crucial. What's considered polite in one culture may be seen as offensive in another. For instance, in many Western cultures, direct eye contact is respectful, but in some Asian cultures, it may be perceived as aggressive. Being aware of these differences and adapting your communication style is key to fostering positive relationships and avoiding misunderstandings in cross-cultural interactions.

Mastering effective communication also involves becoming a skilled storyteller. Anecdotes and well-chosen narratives make your points more relatable, memorable, and engaging. A well-crafted story can vividly illustrate your ideas, capture attention and leave a lasting impression. The key is to keep stories concise and relevant to your message, avoiding unnecessary tangents.

Developing strong communication skills is an ongoing process. It's not just about speaking eloquently but understanding your audience, adapting your message, and ensuring your communication is clear and impactful. By paying attention to word choice, tone, body language, and cultural context, you can express yourself with clarity and grace, leaving a positive, lasting impression.

Effective communication also plays a critical role in professional settings. In business, clear, concise communication is essential for conveying information, making persuasive arguments, and building consensus. Ambiguity can lead to misunderstandings, missed deadlines, and project failures. Professionals who communicate well are valued for their ability to articulate ideas, so listen actively, and navigate complex situations with composure.

In presenting a business proposal, clarity is paramount. Start with a concise summary of the main points, then elaborate on each with clear, simple language. Avoid technical jargon unless it's familiar to the audience. Support your claims with data and evidence, using visual aids like charts or graphs to make the information more digestible. Maintain eye contact, modulate your tone, and use body language to engage the audience. Allow time for questions and respond thoughtfully.

The same principles apply to written communication. Whether it's emails, memos, or reports, clarity is key. Avoid ambiguity, use a professional tone, and proofread to eliminate errors that can undermine your credibility. Written communication requires more precision as there are no nonverbal cues to support your message.

In summary, effective communication is a multifaceted skill that goes beyond simply speaking or writing. It involves mastering active listening, choosing your words carefully, modulating your tone, using appropriate body language, and understanding cultural context. By refining these elements, you can craft clear, impactful messages that resonate with your audience and achieve your goals. This mastery will improve your interactions in both social and professional settings, fostering stronger relationships and greater success.

Consistent practice, along with a willingness to adapt and refine your approach, will transform the ability to express yourself with clarity and grace. The journey toward becoming an effective communicator is lifelong, rewarding those who invest in it with continually improved outcomes.

Engaging Others through Narrative

The ability to weave a compelling narrative is a cornerstone of engaging conversation. It's not about dominating the discussion with lengthy monologues, but rather using carefully selected anecdotes and observations to illustrate a point, add depth, or simply create a more memorable experience for everyone involved. Storytelling in conversation is about painting vivid pictures with words, building an emotional connection with your listener, and leaving a lasting impression.

Mastering this art requires more than recounting events; it's about crafting a narrative that is both concise and engaging. Think of it as a miniature work of nonfiction, structured to maximize its impact. This involves several key techniques.

First, consider the structure of your story. A well-crafted anecdote typically follows a clear narrative arc, even if it's brief. Start with a captivating hook, such as something surprising, a provocative question, or a statement that piques the listener's interest. This draws them in and compels them to want more.

For instance, instead of saying, "I had a difficult business trip last month," try, "The flight attendant's announcement about unexpected turbulence was only the beginning of what turned out to be a truly memorable trip to Hong Kong." This immediately sparks intrigue and invites further questions.

Next, build the narrative by providing relevant details without overwhelming your listener with unnecessary information. Focus on the key elements that contribute to the story's overall impact and leave out the less important ones. Think of it like a sculptor chiseling away excess material to reveal the essence of the story.

Your details should be vivid and sensory. Instead of saying, "The food was good," describe the experience: "The aroma of freshly baked bread filled the air as I sat down, and the first bite of pasta was a symphony of flavors: creamy, rich, and subtly spiced." Use descriptive language to evoke sights, sounds, smells, tastes, and textures to paint a clear picture in the listener's mind.

Show don't tell. Instead of simply stating your emotions ("I was very nervous"), demonstrate them through actions and details ("My hands were shaking as I walked onto the stage, and my throat felt like sandpaper"). This allows the listener to feel the experience, making it more powerful and relatable.

The pacing of your story is also crucial. Vary the rhythm of your speech, using pauses for emphasis and building suspense. Don't rush through the story; allow your listener time to absorb the information and engage with the narrative.

The climax of your story, the most exciting or significant moment should be delivered with impact. This is where the core message or lesson of the story becomes clear. In the Hong Kong business trip example, the climax might be a critical negotiation, an unexpected problem-solving moment, or a surprising encounter.

Conclude your story with a concise and memorable closing statement. This might be a reflection on the experience, a lesson learned, or a connection back to the original topic of conversation. A well-crafted ending solidifies the narrative's impact, leaving a lasting impression.

Remember, the goal is not to impress with elaborate tales but to connect with your listener. Authenticity is key; share genuine and relevant stories, avoiding embellishments or exaggerations. A simple, well-told personal story often resonates more than an overly complex narrative.

Storytelling goes beyond personal anecdotes. Observational skills are just as valuable. The ability to notice intriguing details around you and share those observations can enrich a conversation. For example, you could share an insightful observation about a building's architectural style, the behavior of people in a setting, or a surprising natural phenomenon.

Sharpening your observational skills requires practice. Pay attention to subtle shifts in body language, tone, or behavior. Practice translating these details into evocative descriptions, which can lead to surprisingly insightful and engaging conversational moments.

Additionally, connecting your observations to broader themes enhances their significance. A specific observation can be tied to a historical trend, a current news story, or a classic literary reference, adding depth to your contribution and demonstrating your intellectual curiosity.

For example, if you observe a street musician playing a melancholic tune, instead of simply commenting on their talent, you might note how the somber mood of the music contrasts with the bustling surroundings, perhaps linking it to urban isolation. This adds a social or cultural context, enriching the conversation.

Another example could involve observing how people interact at a gathering. You might notice how small groups are engaged in intense conversations, perhaps suggesting a shift in social dynamics due to the prevalence of cellular phones. Alternatively, you could draw a parallel to historical accounts of social interactions in specific settings.

The ability to tell stories and share insightful observations is a crucial element of conversation. It's not just about relaying information; it's about creating an experience, building connections, and leaving a lasting impression. With careful structuring, vivid descriptions, and a genuine desire to connect, you can turn ordinary conversations into memorable interactions that enrich your relationships and expand your influence.

Honing these skills will make you a more engaging and captivating conversationalist, effortlessly captivating your audience and leaving a positive impression. This skill, cultivated through practice and observation, contributes to a life well lived. The rewards extend beyond casual conversations, enhancing professional relationships and ultimately enriching your overall life experience.

Diplomacy and Tact

Navigating difficult conversations is an essential skill in both professional and personal settings. Whether addressing performance issues with a colleague or mediating a disagreement among friends, the key to handling these delicate situations lies in diplomacy and tact. These qualities demonstrate respect for others and a commitment to constructive dialogue. Mastering the art of difficult conversations requires preparation, active listening, and emotional intelligence.

Preparation is paramount before engaging in a challenging conversation. Clarify your objectives: What outcome do you hope to achieve? What key points need to be conveyed, and how can you do so clearly and concisely? Anticipate the other person's perspective, understanding their viewpoint allows you to address potential objections thoughtfully. This isn't about expecting agreement, but rather acknowledging concerns and formulating responses that are preemptively constructive.

The physical setting also plays a crucial role. Choose a space that promotes privacy and fosters comfort and trust. A quiet office or a neutral, distraction-free area is ideal. Avoid public spaces where interruptions are possible, and focus on creating an atmosphere conducive to open communication, free from external pressures.

Once the setting is established, begin the conversation with a calm and respectful tone. Acknowledge the other person's perspective, even if you disagree, and validate their feelings. Statements like, "I understand this is frustrating," or "I can see why you feel this way," help create a constructive atmosphere. Avoid accusatory language or interruptions, instead practice active listening. Pay attention to both verbal and nonverbal cues. These subtle signals often offer insights into the person's emotions and concerns, enabling you to address their feelings more effectively.

Active listening goes beyond hearing words because it requires engagement. Ask clarifying questions to ensure you fully understand their perspective. Summarize their points periodically to confirm comprehension, which shows attentiveness and helps prevent misunderstandings. Rephrasing their concerns in your own words not only demonstrates active listening but also diffuses tension, creating a space where both parties feel heard before discussing solutions.

When it's your turn to speak, maintain composure and express your views clearly and directly. Frame your points in a constructive way, focusing on collaboration rather than assigning blame. "Use 'I' statements to express your feelings without sounding accusatory. For example, instead of saying, 'You always interrupt me,' try, 'I feel unheard when interrupted.' This shifts the conversation from blame to understanding.[4]"

Be mindful of nonverbal communication throughout the conversation. Maintain eye contact, use open body language, and avoid defensive or aggressive gestures. These nonverbal cues convey respect and attentiveness, and can significantly influence the overall tone of the interaction.

Diplomacy also involves flexibility. Be prepared to adjust your approach based on the person's reactions and the conversation's dynamics. At times, you may need to pause, take a deep breath and reassess your strategy. The goal isn't to "win" the argument, but to reach a mutually beneficial resolution. A willingness to compromise can open doors to constructive solutions.

Mastering difficult conversations is a crucial life skill. It requires preparation, emotional intelligence, active listening, and a commitment to respectful dialogue. By honing these skills, you can turn challenging interactions into opportunities for understanding and positive outcomes. The goal is not to change someone's mind, but to foster mutual respect and collaboration.

Not every difficult conversation will have an immediate resolution. Sometimes, the most effective strategy is to acknowledge the complexity of the issue and agree to revisit it later. This gives both parties time to process, gather insights, or cool down, especially when emotions run high. Forcing a resolution prematurely can be counterproductive.

Consider the long-term impact of the conversation. Will the resolution strengthen your relationship or create distance? These considerations should guide your approach and decisions. Navigating challenging conversations gracefully is an investment in the quality of your professional and personal relationships.

In addition, cultivating self-awareness is essential. Understand your own emotional responses and triggers to manage difficult conversations effectively. Reflect on your communication style. Do you tend to interrupt or become defensive? Being aware of these tendencies allows you to adjust your behavior, leading to more constructive outcomes. Recognizing your personal biases is equally important, as they can influence your interpretation of the conversation and the other person's behavior.

Difficult conversations are learned skills, honed over time with practice and reflection. Each experience offers a chance to refine your approach. Consider journaling to track your conversations. By analyzing successes and challenges you can identify areas for improvement. This self-reflection ensures continuous growth in your communication abilities.

Finally, empathy plays a pivotal role. Putting yourself in the other person's shoes fosters understanding, reduces defensiveness, and promotes a collaborative atmosphere. Empathy isn't about agreeing with the other person. It's about recognizing and respecting their perspective. By practicing empathy, you create a pathway for respectful and constructive dialogue, which is often the first step toward resolution.

Navigating difficult conversations is a vital skill that strengthens relationships and fosters positive outcomes. It's a continuous learning process that contributes to both personal growth and better interactions with others.

Establishing Meaningful Connections

Building genuine connections is more than just exchanging pleasantries; it's about establishing a rapport that fosters mutual respect and understanding. This process, vital in both professional and personal spheres, relies on active listening, genuine interest, and thoughtful engagement. It's about moving beyond superficial interactions to create meaningful relationships based on shared experiences and respect. The ability to build rapport is a skill developed over time, requiring practice, self-awareness, and a willingness to connect on a deeper level.

One of the most effective ways to build rapport is by discovering shared interests. This doesn't mean finding someone with the exact same passions, but identify common ground, no matter how small. It might be a shared love for a particular music genre, a favorite sport, or a mutual appreciation for an author or film. This commonality provides an immediate connection, offering a springboard for conversation and the foundation for familiarity and camaraderie.

Identifying shared interests often starts with attentive listening. Pay close attention to what the other person says, to both their words and the tone, body language, and subtle cues that reveal their interests and values. Are they passionate about their work? Do they mention hobbies or activities outside of work? Do they express opinions about current events or trends? These seemingly minor details collectively provide a clearer picture of the individual and suggest potential avenues for connection.

Once a shared interest is identified, engage thoughtfully. This means moving beyond surface-level agreement. Instead, delve deeper into the subject by asking open-ended questions that invite the other person to elaborate on their thoughts and feelings. For example, if you find a shared interest in vintage cars, avoid simply saying, "I like vintage cars too." Ask questions like, "What is it about vintage cars that you find most appealing? Do you have a favorite model or era?" These questions show genuine interest and encourage the other person to share their passion, which strengthens the connection. Furthermore, actively listening to their responses, asking follow-up questions, and making related observations will deepen the bond.

Let the conversation flow naturally, avoiding forced or contrived topics. Authenticity is key. If you're genuinely interested, your enthusiasm will be contagious, encouraging the other person to reciprocate. The goal is to create a comfortable, engaging atmosphere where both parties feel at ease sharing their thoughts and feelings. Avoid dominating the conversation; instead, aim for a balanced exchange of ideas. Remember, a conversation is not a competition, but an opportunity to build a genuine connection.

Building rapport also involves demonstrating empathy and understanding. Even if you don't share the same passions, actively listening and acknowledging the other person's perspective is crucial. This means not just hearing their words but understanding the emotions and motivations behind them. It involves recognizing their feelings and validating their experiences, even if you wouldn't react the same way in a similar situation.

Empathy is especially important in professional settings. Understanding the challenges and perspectives of colleagues and clients allows you to communicate more effectively and build stronger relationships. By demonstrating empathy, you create trust and show that you value the other person's thoughts and feelings. This is particularly valuable in conflict resolution, where understanding the other party's perspective is key to finding common ground and resolving disputes amicably.

In business, building rapport is essential for successful negotiations and collaborations. When people feel understood and respected, they are more likely to be receptive to your ideas and willing to compromise. Actively listening and responding with genuine empathy help build trust and establish productive relationships. This applies not only to negotiations but also to everyday interactions with colleagues, clients, and supervisors. The more rapport you build, the smoother professional interactions become, leading to greater efficiency and understanding.

Beyond shared interests, finding common ground can also involve shared values or experiences. Perhaps you both volunteer for a similar charity, have visited the same place, or share similar views on a social issue. These experiences can lead to deeper conversations and a stronger connection. It's important to recognize that these connections don't always need to be overt; often, it's the unspoken understanding that builds strong rapport.

Nonverbal communication also plays a significant role in building rapport. Maintaining appropriate eye contact, offering a genuine smile, and using open body language all contribute to a welcoming atmosphere. These cues signal openness and approachability. Conversely, closed-off body language, like crossed arms or avoiding eye contact can create barriers. Be mindful of your body language, ensure it reflects your genuine interest and desire to connect.

Building rapport is not just a technique to be mechanically applied; it's a process of genuine connection that requires sincerity, patience, and a willingness to engage with others on their terms. Authenticity is vital. Insincere attempts at building rapport are easily detected and can damage potential relationships. Your efforts must be genuine, reflecting a true desire to connect and understand the other person.

Finally, remember that building rapport is an ongoing process, not a one-time event. Meaningful relationships are cultivated over time through consistent effort and genuine engagement. Regularly seek opportunities to connect with others, actively listen to their perspectives, and show a genuine interest in their lives. By consistently practicing these principles, you will not only build stronger relationships but also enrich your personal and professional life. These connections create a sense of belonging and contribute to a richer, more fulfilling life. The investment you make in building rapport is an investment in yourself and your future, with substantial, long-lasting rewards. Cultivating this skill is foundational for both personal growth and professional success.

Chapter 3

Business Etiquette – Protocol and Professionalism

Making a Positive First Impression in Business

The handshake. A seemingly simple gesture, yet it holds immense power in the world of business. It serves as the often unspoken first impression, setting the tone for the entire interaction. A firm, confident handshake can project authority and trustworthiness, instantly establishing rapport and conveying professionalism. Conversely, a weak, limp, or overly aggressive handshake can undermine your credibility before you've even spoken. Mastering the art of the professional handshake is not just about politeness; it's a crucial skill that can significantly impact your success in business.

The ideal handshake is a balanced blend of firmness and warmth. Avoid a bone-crushing grip that could cause discomfort; this aggressive approach is rarely appreciated and may be interpreted as domineering. Likewise, a limp handshake conveys a lack of confidence and suggests disinterest, instantly diminishing your perceived authority. The goal is to project self-assurance without being overbearing. A firm but gentle pressure, paired with appropriate eye contact and a genuine smile, creates a positive first

CHAPTER 3

impression with lasting impact.

The process begins even before physical contact. As you approach the other person, maintain a confident posture: stand tall, shoulders relaxed, and offer a warm, genuine smile. Avoid fidgeting or showing nervous habits, as these nonverbal cues can detract from your confidence. When extending your hand, make eye contact. A direct gaze shows respect and confidence, indicating you're present and engaged. However, be cautious not to stare intensely; maintaining natural, comfortable eye contact is key.

The grip itself is critical. Extend your hand fully, but avoid reaching across the table or overextending your arm. The ideal grip is firm yet comfortable but it's a pressure that conveys confidence and respect. A handshake should last about two to three seconds. Any shorter duration may feel abrupt or dismissive, while a longer handshake can be awkward. During the handshake, maintain eye contact and offer a brief professional greeting such as, "It's a pleasure to meet you," or "Good to see you again." A genuine smile further reinforces the positive impression you're trying to create.

Beyond the mechanics, context is crucial. Consider the setting and the person you're greeting. In formal business settings, like a job interview or high-stakes meeting, the handshake should be particularly professional and measured. In informal settings, it may be slightly less formal, but professionalism should still be maintained. Adapt your handshake to the individual, being mindful of cultural norms. In some cultures, a prolonged handshake or light touch on the arm is appropriate, while in others, a brief, firm handshake is preferred. Demonstrating sensitivity to cultural nuances shows respect and understanding.

Let's explore the handshake in specific situations. At a networking event, surrounded by potential clients or colleagues, the handshake becomes an essential tool for building rapport. It's not just about the physical action; it's the interaction as a whole. Your body language from your posture, smile to your eye contact will all contribute to the impression you make. Aim for a confident yet approachable demeanor, introduce yourself clearly, and remember the other person's name. A brief, engaging conversation following a strong handshake can pave the way for a fruitful business relationship.

Consider a job interview scenario, where the handshake carries even greater weight. It's one of the first things the interviewer will notice, setting the tone for the entire conversation. A strong, confident handshake conveys self-assurance and professionalism, both highly valued traits. Avoid an overly enthusiastic handshake, which might come across as insincere or desperate. Instead, aim for a steady, firm grip that reflects your maturity and professionalism.

But what about those tricky situations when the handshake deviates from the norm? If someone offers a weak handshake, don't draw attention to it. Simply respond with a firm yet gentle grip, ensuring your handshake maintains professionalism while respecting their style. Similarly, if you encounter an overly aggressive handshake, stay calm and composed. Adjust your grip to a comfortable level without making it an issue. The key is to navigate these situations with grace and professionalism to maintain a smooth interaction.

Hygiene is another critical aspect. Ensure your hands are clean and dry before offering a handshake. Nothing undermines professionalism like a clammy, unclean hand. In professional settings, hygiene plays a pivotal role in conveying both professionalism and consideration. Take the time to wash your hands thoroughly and, if needed, use lotion to avoid dryness. A well-maintained appearance, starting with clean hands, is crucial for projecting a polished image.

Understanding the unspoken language of the handshake can also reveal valuable insights into a person's character. While not an infallible indicator, a firm handshake can suggest qualities like self-assurance, decisiveness, and professionalism. Conversely, a weak or hesitant handshake might imply timidity or a lack of confidence, though this can also be influenced by cultural differences or personal preferences. Observing these nonverbal cues helps you better understand the dynamics of your interactions and fine-tune your approach.

In summary, the professional handshake is more than just a greeting; it's a powerful tool for communication, projecting professionalism and building rapport. It's an art form that requires practice and awareness. By mastering the mechanics, understanding its nuances, and adapting your approach to different situations, you'll cultivate a valuable asset that enhances your professional interactions. This simple gesture has a significant impact and is a foundational element of business etiquette. Perfect your handshake and you'll be well on your way to making a lasting, positive impression in the business world. Remember, the impression you make could be the difference between securing a deal or establishing a long-term professional relationship.

Building Relationships in Professional Settings

Building genuine connections in the professional sphere is less about collecting business cards and more about cultivating meaningful relationships. When done effectively, networking transcends the transactional; it's about forging authentic bonds rooted in mutual respect and shared interests. The key is moving beyond superficial exchanges and engaging in conversations that uncover common ground and build real rapport.

Conferences and networking events provide fertile ground for cultivating connections. However, the sheer volume of people and the often frantic energy can feel overwhelming. The trick is to approach these events strategically, with a clear plan and a mindset focused on quality over quantity. Before attending, research the guest list or speaker lineup. Identify individuals whose expertise aligns with your professional goals or whose work resonates with you. This research allows you to approach conversations with informed curiosity, making your interactions more engaging and memorable

Rather than trying to speak to everyone, prioritize quality engagement with a select few. Aim for deeper conversations with individuals who genuinely pique your interest, rather than flitting from person to person and exchanging fleeting pleasantries. The art of conversation is central to effective networking. Practice active listening, demonstrating a genuine interest in what others have to say. Ask open-ended questions that encourage thoughtful responses and reveal shared perspectives. Avoid dominating the conversation; strive for a balanced exchange of ideas. Remember the power of the pause. Allowing silence to breathe into the conversation can often lead to deeper insights and more authentic connections.

Your body language plays a crucial role in conveying your engagement and sincerity. Maintain appropriate eye contact, offer a warm smile, and adopt an open posture. These nonverbal cues communicate confidence and approachability, encouraging others to engage with you. On the flip side, crossed arms or an averted gaze can project disinterest or defensiveness, hindering building rapport.

Following up after a conference or networking event is essential for solidifying relationships. Send personalized emails to individuals you connected with, referencing something specific from your conversation. This shows you were genuinely attentive and not just collecting contacts. A simple, well-crafted email acknowledging a shared interest or reiterating a point discussed can go a long way in nurturing a professional relationship. Avoid generic, mass-produced emails; personalized messages reflect genuine interest and are far more likely to elicit a positive response.

Online networking platforms like LinkedIn also offer valuable opportunities to build professional connections. However, it's crucial to cultivate a thoughtful and authentic digital presence. Your LinkedIn profile should reflect your professional identity accurately and be engaging. Avoid generic summaries; instead, craft a compelling narrative that showcases your unique skills and experiences. Regularly engage with relevant content and contribute thoughtful comments to discussions, demonstrating your expertise and fostering meaningful interactions with others in your field.

Remember, networking is a long-term endeavor, not a quick fix. Building strong professional relationships requires consistent effort and genuine engagement. Nurturing these connections over time through periodic emails, informational interviews, or attending industry events is essential for cultivating a supportive professional network. Think of networking like gardening: consistent attention and nurturing are needed to cultivate strong, fruitful relationships.

Consider leveraging your existing network. Informational interviews with people already working in fields of interest can provide invaluable insights and potential connections. These meetings are not about asking for a job but rather about learning, exploring possibilities, and building rapport with professionals who can offer guidance and support. Approach these interviews with a prepared list of insightful questions that demonstrate your interest and preparedness. Express sincere gratitude for their time and offer to reciprocate in some way; perhaps by sharing relevant information or connecting them with someone in your network to further solidify the relationship.

Professional organizations and industry associations provide another excellent avenue for networking. Membership often grants access to exclusive events, networking opportunities, and publications, enabling you to connect with like-minded professionals. Actively participate in the organization's activities, such as attending meetings, volunteering, and contributing to discussions. This not only increases your visibility but also demonstrates your commitment to the field and fosters relationships with colleagues who share your interests.

Networking isn't just about self-promotion; it's about a reciprocal exchange. Be genuinely interested in others, actively listen to their perspectives, and offer assistance where appropriate. By approaching networking with a mindset of mutual benefit, you'll not only build strong professional relationships but also establish yourself as a valuable member of your community.

Beyond structured networking events, there are informal opportunities to cultivate relationships. Lunch meetings with colleagues, attending industry conferences, or even casual conversations at professional gatherings can yield surprising results. These informal interactions often lead to more relaxed and genuine conversations, facilitating deeper connections. Be mindful of your body language and conversational style; your demeanor greatly influences the impressions you make.

One often overlooked aspect of networking is the power of mentorship. Seeking out mentors within your field can provide invaluable guidance, support, and career advice. Mentorship is a two-way street, requiring mutual respect and a commitment to reciprocal growth. Identify professionals whose careers you admire and whose values align with your own. Approach them respectfully, expressing admiration for their work and requesting a meeting to discuss their career path. Be prepared with thoughtful questions, and remember that the goal is to learn, not to demand favors.

Expanding your network also involves staying updated on industry news and trends. Subscribing to relevant publications, attending webinars, and engaging in online discussions allows you to remain informed and contribute meaningfully to conversations with colleagues. Sharing insightful articles or commenting thoughtfully on industry news demonstrates your engagement and willingness to participate, helping you foster connections with others who share your interests.

Finally, authenticity is key. Trying to project a persona that isn't truly reflective of yourself will backfire. Genuine engagement and honest communication are the cornerstones of lasting relationships. By being yourself and expressing sincere enthusiasm and interest, you'll create far more meaningful connections than by relying on superficial tactics. When practiced authentically and thoughtfully, networking becomes a powerful tool for building a strong and supportive professional network, paving the way for a fulfilling and successful career. The ultimate success of networking lies not in the number of contacts amassed but, in the depth, and quality of the relationships forged. By cultivating genuine connections, you'll not only build a network but a community of support and collaboration that will enhance your professional trajectory immeasurably.

Punctuality and Professional Demeanor

Punctuality is the cornerstone of professional success. Arriving late to a meeting, regardless of the reason, sends the message of disorganization and a lack of respect for others' time. It suggests that you don't value the agenda, or the individuals involved, which undermines your credibility before you even speak. In today's fast-paced business environment, time is precious, and punctuality shows you respect both your own time and that of your colleagues. The ripple effect of lateness is significant: a delayed meeting disrupts schedules and leads to lost productivity for everyone involved. The initial impression of unprofessionalism can be difficult, if not impossible, to overcome.

However, punctuality goes beyond just arriving on time. It's about being well-prepared in advance. This means reviewing the agenda, gathering necessary materials, and mentally preparing your contributions before the scheduled meeting time. Such proactive preparation underscores your seriousness and commitment, setting a positive tone for the meeting. Moreover, it allows you to actively engage in discussions, rather than scrambling to catch up, which leads to more productive exchanges of ideas.

Preparation also includes logistical considerations. Do you know the location? Have you accounted for possible traffic delays or unforeseen circumstances? Planning for contingencies shows foresight and dedication to the meeting's success. This attention to detail transcends punctuality, showcasing a responsible, proactive attitude that is invaluable in any professional setting. It's a subtle yet powerful way to demonstrate respect for others' time and your dedication to the task at hand.

Appropriate attire plays a crucial role in conveying professionalism and respect. While dress codes will vary by industry, company culture, and the nature of the meeting, the underlying principle remains the same: dress in a way that shows respect for the occasion and those present. It's not necessarily about rigid formality but about making a conscious effort to present yourself appropriately. In most cases, a smart-casual approach, such as a neat, well-fitting clothing that conveys confidence and competence strikes a good balance.

The context matters too. A meeting with potential investors calls for a more formal approach than a casual brainstorming session with colleagues. But even in less formal settings, attention to detail is important. Neatness, cleanliness, and proper grooming are key components of a professional appearance. Wrinkled clothing, unkempt hair, or distracting accessories can detract from your message and damage your credibility. The goal isn't to stand out ostentatiously but to present yourself in a manner that aligns with your professional demeanor and the message you want to convey.

Grooming also plays a significant role. Well-maintained hair, clean nails, and a subtle scent contribute to the overall impression you make. These details reflect your attention to personal discipline and professional attitude. While overt displays of grooming products should be avoided, a polished appearance communicates that you care about how you present yourself and, by extension, how you present your ideas and work.

Professional conduct during the meeting itself is just as important. Active listening is crucial. It shows respect for the speaker and demonstrates your genuine engagement. Avoid interrupting, even if you have something important to say. Wait for a natural pause and then share your thoughts. Maintaining eye contact indicates attentiveness, while mindful body language, avoiding fidgeting or slouching, projects confidence and professionalism.

Respectful disagreement is another key aspect of professional conduct. While it's important to express your views, it's essential to do so with courtesy and consideration. Avoid aggressive language or personal attacks. Instead, focus on the issues at hand and express your disagreements constructively. This approach shows your ability to engage in healthy debate, a valuable skill in any collaborative setting. Effective communication involves not just expressing your own opinions but also understanding and appreciating others' perspectives.

Being mindful of group dynamics is equally important. Avoid dominating the conversation and allow others to contribute their thoughts. This fosters a more inclusive, collaborative atmosphere, demonstrating respect for everyone's input. Active listening and thoughtful responses are vital for an equitable exchange of ideas.

The use of technology during meetings also requires careful consideration. Ensure your phone is silenced or turned off to avoid disruptive notifications. If you're using a laptop or tablet, minimize distractions and focus on the discussion at hand. Thoughtful use of technology reflects your respect for others' time and attention. Disruptions can easily derail a meeting, so being mindful of how you engage with technology is a crucial element of professionalism.

Finally, don't overlook the importance of a graceful exit. Before leaving, thank the attendees for their time and contributions. Summarize key takeaways and action items, reinforcing the value of the meeting and your commitment to follow-up. A courteous farewell leaves a lasting positive impression, helping to close the meeting on a note of professionalism and respect.

In conclusion, mastering meeting etiquette goes far beyond simply arriving on time. It's about a comprehensive approach that prioritizes punctuality, preparedness, appropriate attire, professional conduct, and careful use of technology. By paying attention to these details, you demonstrate respect for others, a commitment to the meeting's objectives, and professional competence. The cumulative effect of consistently displaying these qualities will help build your reputation as a reliable and professional individual, paving the way for career advancement and stronger relationships. It's a subtle art, but one that pays substantial dividends in both professional success and personal satisfaction.

Maintaining Professional Standards

The transition from face-to-face interactions to digital communication requires a refined understanding of professional etiquette. While the core principles of respect and consideration remain constant, the nuances of digital communication demand a different approach. Email, in particular, has become the primary mode of professional interaction, balancing the formality of letters with the informality of casual conversations. Mastering this medium is essential for projecting a professional image and fostering positive working relationships.

The first key element in professional email communication is clarity. Ambiguity has no place in email correspondence. Ensure your message is concise, focused, and easy to understand. Avoid jargon, overly complex sentences, and excessive acronyms. Keep in mind that the recipient may not be familiar with your industry's specific terminology, so aim for universal comprehension. Before hitting "send", reread your email for potential misinterpretations or areas where clarity can be improved. A well-structured email, one with a clear subject line, a brief introduction, focused body text, and a concluding paragraph, makes for better understanding and reduces the chances of miscommunication.

Tone is equally important in email. Without nonverbal cues to guide interpretation, sarcasm, wit, and humor can be easily misinterpreted. Maintain a consistently professional and respectful tone, even when dealing with complex or challenging situations. Avoid overly informal language, such as slang or colloquialisms. Use formal salutations ("Dear Mr./Ms. [Last Name]") and professional closings ("Sincerely", "Regards", "Kind regards"). The closing you choose subtly influences the level of formality, so be mindful of your relationship with the recipient and the context of the communication.

Proofreading is non-negotiable. Typos, grammatical errors, and spelling mistakes undermine your credibility and suggest a lack of attention to detail. Before sending any email, carefully review it for such errors. Use your word processor's spell check and grammar check functions, but don't rely solely on them. A second reading with fresh eyes is essential. For particularly important emails, consider asking a colleague to proofread them, especially when sending messages to clients or senior management. The time spent on proofreading is an investment in your professional reputation.

In addition to writing mechanics, consider the content itself. Ensure that your email is relevant, concise, and focused on the subject matter. Avoid including unnecessary information or irrelevant details. Respect the recipient's time by keeping your emails brief and to the point. Organize your thoughts logically, using bullet points or numbered lists when appropriate to improve readability. Overly long emails can overwhelm the recipient and decrease the likelihood of your message being fully understood or acted upon. If a lengthy communication is necessary, consider breaking it into smaller, more digestible emails.

Email etiquette also extends to attachments. Always indicate the purpose of any attachments in the body of your email, and ensure that the files are appropriately named and easy to download. Avoid sending excessively large attachments that may slow down the recipient's email system or require them to use special software. Compressing files or providing a lower-resolution version are considerate alternatives. Additionally, always check the security of any files you share through email, especially when dealing with sensitive or confidential information.

The promptness of your replies is another crucial aspect of digital communication. Responding to emails in a timely manner demonstrates respect for your colleagues and clients. Aim to respond within 24 hours, or sooner if the matter is urgent. If you anticipate a delay in your response, inform the sender and provide an estimated timeframe for when they can expect a reply. This simple act of communication prevents unnecessary anxiety and upholds professionalism.

Digital communication extends beyond email. Instant messaging platforms, social media, and professional networking sites all require adherence to professional standards. Even in these more informal settings, clarity and a professional tone are crucial. Avoid using slang, emojis, or overly casual language. Be mindful of your online presence, ensuring your profiles present a professional image that aligns with your career aspirations. Think before posting anything online because your digital footprint can have long-lasting implications for your professional life.

On professional networking platforms like LinkedIn, maintain a consistent professional persona. Your profile should accurately reflect your skills, experience, and accomplishments in a concise and impactful manner. Engage with other professionals respectfully, and remember that your online interactions can influence your reputation. Participating in relevant discussions and sharing insightful content positions you as a thoughtful professional in your field.

CHAPTER 3

Social media use in a professional context requires careful consideration. While platforms like Twitter and Instagram can be valuable networking tools, the line between personal and professional can blur quickly. Avoid sharing sensitive information or opinions that could reflect poorly on your employer or profession. Be aware that your online activity is often visible to a wider audience than anticipated, so maintain a professional image in all your digital interactions.

Mastering the art of professional digital communication requires consistent effort. It's not just about avoiding mistakes; it's more about projecting a professional image, building rapport, and fostering positive working relationships. By following these guidelines, you'll enhance your professional reputation and contribute to a more effective and positive communication environment. Adhering to professional digital etiquette, much like punctuality and appropriate attire in face-to-face meetings, is a significant investment that yields substantial returns in your professional life.

Consider the impact of digital communication on your overall professional brand. Every email, message, and online interaction contributes to how others perceive you. Cultivating a digital presence that reflects your professionalism, expertise, and commitment to your field is crucial. Your digital communications often serve as the first impression you make on potential clients, collaborators, or employers. Therefore, careful attention to detail and maintaining high standards of professional communication are indispensable for success.

In summary, the principles of professionalism are timeless, regardless of the medium. While tools and channels may change, the core principles of respect, clarity, and consideration remain paramount. Mastering digital communication etiquette isn't just avoiding mistakes; it's about building a strong professional reputation that extends beyond the digital sphere and reflects your character and competence in all areas of your professional life. Dedication to clear communication, a professional tone, and meticulous attention to detail will shape your reputation as dependable, reliable, and professional. An investment that will pay dividends throughout your career.

Impressing Clients and Colleagues

Business dinners represent a unique blend of professional and social etiquette. These gatherings provide a less formal setting than boardroom meetings but still require a high degree of professionalism and awareness. Mastering the nuances of a successful business dinner can enhance your professional relationships and contribute to your overall success. The key is understanding the unspoken rules of behavior from seating arrangements to the art of conversation.

The initial invitation often sets the tone. A formal invitation, perhaps sent via physical card or a carefully crafted email, indicates a more traditional and formal event. A less formal invitation, such as a phone call or casual email, suggests a more relaxed atmosphere. Regardless of how the invitation is extended, always confirm your attendance promptly and note any dietary restrictions or allergies to avoid potential embarrassment for your host. Punctuality is crucial. Arriving late shows a lack of respect for your host's time and the other attendees.

Seating arrangements are rarely random. Often, the host has a predetermined plan, positioning individuals strategically to facilitate networking and conversation. Pay attention to the seating arrangement and avoid choosing your seat independently. If you're unsure, politely inquire with your host or another knowledgeable individual. The seats closest to the host are usually reserved for senior individuals or the most important guests. This isn't just about protocol; it demonstrates awareness of organizational dynamics and social hierarchy, signaling professionalism and adaptability.

When ordering from the menu, tact and consideration are key. Observe your host's choice before making your selection. If they opt for a moderately priced dish, follow suit; choosing the most expensive item may appear ostentatious or inconsiderate. Avoid complicated or messy dishes that could be difficult to eat gracefully. Consider the dietary restrictions and preferences of your colleagues and clients, and inquire thoughtfully about any allergies or preferences. Limiting alcohol consumption is also important because excessive drinking can undermine your professional image and impair your judgment. Choose still or sparkling water or a single glass of wine unless the host indicates otherwise.

As the meal progresses, conversation becomes a central component of the evening. The dinner table is not only for eating but for fostering connections and building rapport. Engage in polite conversation, showing genuine interest in your colleagues and clients. Steer clear of controversial topics, such as politics or religion, which can easily derail a discussion and create tension. Focus on mutual interests, such as industry trends, recent news, or shared experiences. Practice active listening, responding appropriately and avoiding interrupting others. This is your chance to showcase your communication skills, not just your dining etiquette.

Maintaining proper table manners is essential. Keep your elbows off the table, use cutlery properly, and refrain from speaking with your mouth full. These small details project professionalism and refinement. While informality may be encouraged in some settings, it's important to maintain the decorum appropriate for a business dinner. This doesn't mean being stiff or unnatural, but rather demonstrating mindfulness and respect for others.

The business dinner continues beyond the meal itself. Afterward, the conversation often continues informally, offering an opportunity to strengthen relationships and address any remaining concerns. Offer to assist with the bill or graciously accept if the host insists on covering it. Always express gratitude to the host for their hospitality, reinforcing your appreciation for the opportunity to connect. A handwritten thank-you note sent the next day further solidifies your professionalism and thoughtfulness.

Networking is another essential aspect of a successful business dinner. This is an opportunity to build connections and strengthen existing relationships. Engage in meaningful conversations, remember names, and show genuine interest in what others share. This isn't just about collecting business cards but more about building authentic relationships. Following up on any commitments made during the dinner shows accountability and professionalism.

Handling unexpected situations with composure is equally important. Whether it's a spilled drink, an awkward silence, or a controversial comment, remain calm and professional. Address any mishap with poise and humor to prevent minor incidents from derailing the atmosphere. If a conversation becomes contentious or uncomfortable, subtly redirect it toward a more appropriate and productive topic. Such moments reveal much about your ability to navigate social complexities, a highly valuable skill in the business world. Your calmness in these instances demonstrates emotional intelligence, a key asset in professional environments.

Choosing appropriate attire is also crucial. While a suit may be standard in some business cultures, always consider the context. A jacket and dress pants or business casual attire may be suitable in a less formal setting. Your attire should reflect respect for the event and the people attending. Avoid anything too casual or flashy. Cleanliness and attention to detail in your appearance reflects professionalism and an eye for the finer details. Your overall appearance should complement your professional demeanor, enhancing your reputation.

In conclusion, mastering the etiquette of business dinners is an invaluable skill for any professional. It's not just about knowing how to use cutlery correctly. You need to understand social dynamics, demonstrate respect for colleagues and clients, and create an environment conducive to strong professional relationships. By grasping the nuances of seating arrangements, ordering, conversation, and post-dinner interactions, you can navigate these important events with confidence, leaving a lasting impression of professionalism and grace. A successful business dinner reflects your ability to combine professional expertise with refined social skills, as a testament to your commitment to excellence in all aspects of your career. Investing in mastering these skills will yield significant returns, helping you build a strong network of professional connections. Remember, these events are more than just meals. They are opportunities to build bridges, foster collaborations, and strengthen relationships that can propel your career forward.

Chapter 4

Social Etiquette – Grace and Refinement

Making a Strong First Impression in Social Settings

The ability to make a positive first impression is a cornerstone of social success. It's the subtle art of leaving a lasting, favorable mark that sets the tone for any subsequent interaction. While charm and charisma undoubtedly play a role, the mechanics of a well-executed introduction and greeting are precise and learnable. Mastering these mechanics will provide you with the tools to navigate diverse social settings with confidence and grace.

First impressions are not formed in a single fleeting moment. They are a cumulative effect, built upon a series of carefully considered gestures, words, and even unspoken cues. Your initial handshake, the tone of your voice, posture, and eye contact all contribute to the overall perception others form of you. Each element is a brushstroke on the canvas of your first impression, creating a complete and memorable portrait.

A firm, confident handshake conveys self-assurance and respect. Avoid a limp, lifeless grip that suggests weakness or disinterest, as well as an overly forceful grip that can be perceived as aggressive. The ideal handshake strikes a balance: firm but not forceful, confident but not overbearing. It should be brief, around two to three seconds, allowing for a genuine connection without lingering awkwardly.

Accompanying the handshake is the art of eye contact. Maintain direct eye contact during the handshake and initial exchange of pleasantries. This demonstrates engagement and sincerity, showing that you are fully present. However, prolonged staring can be interpreted as aggressive or unsettling. The key is to find a comfortable balance, holding eye contact for a few seconds at a time, then breaking it naturally. This subtle rhythm of eye contact is a powerful tool in establishing rapport and building trust.

Next, consider your body language. Stand tall with good posture; it projects confidence and self-respect. Maintain an open and approachable stance. Avoid crossed arms or legs, which can signal defensiveness or disinterest. A slight smile enhances your approachability, while subtly mirroring the other person's body language can create a sense of connection and rapport. These nonverbal cues, though often unconscious, are powerful communicators, and mastering them can significantly enhance your ability to make a positive first impression.

The words you choose are equally crucial. Begin with a simple, sincere greeting. "How are you?" or "It's a pleasure to meet you" are classic and always appropriate. In more casual settings, a simple "Hello" or "Hi" suffices. Follow the greeting with a clear and concise introduction of yourself. State your name clearly and enunciate properly. If appropriate, offer a brief context for the introduction, explaining how you know the person you are meeting or how you came to be introduced.

For example, at a networking event, you might say, "It's a pleasure to meet you, Mr. Jones. Sarah Miller mentioned I should connect with you given our shared interest in sustainable business practices." This brief explanation provides context, facilitating a natural and smooth conversation. If introduced in a formal setting, such as a business dinner, a concise introduction is sufficient. Avoid overly long or rambling introductions; brevity and clarity are key.

Introducing others properly is equally important. When introducing two individuals, always mention the more senior person or guest of honor first. For example, if introducing a client to your colleague, say, "Mr. Smith, I'd like to introduce you to my colleague, John Doe." This small act of courtesy shows respect for hierarchy and social norms. In informal settings, you can simply introduce both individuals by name, "Sarah, this is David". Regardless of the setting, ensure both individuals have an opportunity to shake hands and initiate their own conversation.

Navigating introductions and greetings smoothly goes beyond the mechanics of handshakes and verbal pleasantries. It involves cultivating a genuine interest in the person you're meeting. Actively listen, ask thoughtful questions, and show curiosity about their experiences and perspectives. This display of genuine interest transcends the superficiality of a simple exchange, fostering deeper connections and paving the way for positive ongoing relationships.

Cultural context is also important. What is considered an appropriate introduction in one culture might be seen as inappropriate or even offensive in another.[5] Researching common customs and etiquette practices can significantly improve your interactions and demonstrate respect. This extends beyond the handshake to broader aspects of body language, personal space, and conversational etiquette. Sensitivity and awareness toward cultural differences are critical in building rapport and creating positive interactions.

Different settings require different approaches. A formal business meeting demands a different approach than a casual social gathering. In a business context, precision and professionalism are paramount because your introduction should be concise, your handshake firm, and your communication clear and direct. In a more casual setting, a relaxed and informal greeting may be appropriate, but professionalism and respect should still be maintained. Adaptability is key. Adjust your approach depending on the setting and the individuals you are interacting with.

The goal is not simply to complete the ritual of an introduction but to initiate a genuine connection. Approach each introduction as an opportunity to forge a meaningful interaction, one that reflects your character and leaves a positive impression. Authenticity and sincerity are vital; they shine through even in the most carefully crafted introduction, making it truly memorable.

A well-executed introduction and greeting lay the foundation for all further interactions. By mastering the mechanics and cultivating a genuine interest in those you meet, you can transform your social interactions, and create connections that enrich both your personal and professional life. The effort you invest in these seemingly small details can yield significant rewards, solidifying your reputation and fostering meaningful relationships. It's an investment in yourself and in those you choose to surround yourself with. Treat each interaction not as a transaction but as an opportunity for genuine connection.

Beyond the initial introduction, maintaining engagement is crucial. Follow up on shared interests or topics discussed. Remember details such as a person's profession or hobbies, and use them to spark further discussion in subsequent encounters. This demonstrates active listening and genuine interest. Follow-up is especially important in professional contexts, where building rapport can lead to new opportunities and collaborations. A thoughtful follow-up email or phone call is a powerful way to strengthen the initial impression.

Finally, practicing these skills is essential. The more you actively engage in social situations and strive to master these techniques, the more natural and effortless they will become. Attend networking events, join social clubs, or engage in community activities to practice and refine your skills in a low-pressure environment. Do not be discouraged by occasional setbacks; every interaction is a learning opportunity. The more experiences you have, the better you will become at making positive first impressions and forging meaningful connections. The art of social interaction is a continuous journey of refinement and growth.[6] Embrace the process, and the rewards will follow.

Mastering Table Manners and Social Graces

Formal dinners offer a distinctive social experience, requiring a blend of refined table manners and effortless grace. Though the specifics may vary across cultures and settings, the core principles remain consistent: respect for fellow diners, consideration for the overall dining experience, and maintaining composure throughout. Mastering these elements not only enhances your personal image but also strengthens your ability to navigate sophisticated social circles and form meaningful connections.

Let's begin with the foundation: the table setting. The placement of cutlery, glassware, and china follows a set order, often determined by the number of courses. The general rule is to work from the outside in, starting with the utensils placed farthest from your plate for the appetizer, and progressing inward with each successive course. Forks are positioned to the left of the plate, knives to the right, with their blades facing the plate, and spoons to the right of the knives.[7] Wine glasses are typically arranged to the right of the dinner plate, often in decreasing size, reflecting the sequence of wines served. Water glasses, which are larger than wine glasses, are usually placed above the knives. Bread plates are located to the upper left of the dinner plate, with a butter knife resting across the top. While this array may seem overwhelming at first, with practice, it becomes intuitive.

Understanding how to use cutlery is equally important. Hold your fork and knife with a relaxed, yet controlled grip, and avoid clenching them tightly. The American style, which involves cutting small bites at a time, is widely accepted in formal settings. "However, the continental style (where the fork stays in the left hand and the knife in the right throughout the meal) is equally appropriate.[8]" Be mindful to avoid making noise while using your cutlery; keep clinking to a minimum.

The table setting is a carefully choreographed arrangement, and I'm here to guide you through the proper steps. Think of the cutlery, glassware, and china as partners, and I'll show you when and how to engage with them.

In the American style, diners hold the fork in their left hand and the knife in their right while cutting food.[9] After cutting, they switch the fork to the right hand to take a bite, resting the knife on the edge of the plate. To signal that they are still eating, diners place the fork and knife in an inverted V-shape on the plate, with the tines of the fork facing up. Once finished, the fork and knife are placed parallel at the four o'clock position, with the knife blade facing inward and the fork tines facing up.

In the European style, the fork stays in the left hand and the knife in the right throughout the meal.[10] This method is more continuous, with diners maintaining a relaxed, yet refined grip on their cutlery. To signal a pause, the fork and knife are placed at an angle across the plate, with the fork resting at eight o'clock and the knife at four o'clock. The tines of the fork should face downward and the knife blade inward. When finished, both utensils are placed parallel at six o'clock, again with the fork tines facing down.

Now, let's focus on the glassware. In both the American and European styles, wine glasses are arranged in a specific order, typically starting with the largest glass for water and progressing to smaller glasses for white wine, red wine, and dessert wine. In the American style, it's more common for hosts or servers to top up a guest's glass without waiting for a cue, often before it's fully empty. By contrast, the European style often waits for the guest to signal when they'd like a refill, showing respect for their pace and preferences. In formal European dining, a sommelier may pour smaller amounts at a time rather than filling glasses in advance.

As a host or guest at a formal dinner, recognizing the various types of glassware and their specific uses is essential. The most common glasses are for water, red wine, and white wine. The water glass is typically the largest, resembling a goblet, with a capacity of 8 to 12 ounces. In contrast, red and white wine glasses are more refined. The red wine glass features a wider bowl, allowing the wine to breathe and enhancing the release of its complex aromas. The white wine glass, narrower in shape, helps maintain the wine's cooler temperature and directs it to the tip of the tongue to emphasize its acidity.

For special occasions, you might encounter champagne flutes, tall and narrow to preserve the bubbles and crispness of the champagne. Other glassware includes the brandy snifter, with a wide, rounded bowl and short stem, designed to capture the rich aromas of brandy or cognac. The iconic martini glass, with its V-shaped bowl and long stem, is another essential piece, along with the highball glass, a tall, slender tumbler used for mixed drinks and cocktails.

Additionally, there are glasses for after-dinner drinks. The sherry glass, small and tapered, is ideal for sweet or dry sherries, while port wine is often served in a small, narrow glass similar to a red wine glass but smaller in size. Each glass has a unique shape and purpose that enhances the formal dining experience, contributing to the elegance and sophistication of the occasion. Understanding their nuances is key to navigating high-society settings with ease and confidence.

Beyond the physical act of eating, posture and demeanor play a crucial role. Sit upright, with your back straight but relaxed, and avoid slouching or leaning excessively on the table. Engage in polite conversation, but refrain from speaking too loudly or boisterously. Active listening is important: make eye contact and respond thoughtfully to others. Avoid dominating the conversation, allowing others to share their perspectives.

Choosing your words carefully is equally vital. Avoid discussing controversial or sensitive topics such as politics or religion. Instead, steer the conversation toward neutral, pleasant subjects like travel, hobbies, books, or current events, keeping the tone light and engaging. Use respectful language, avoid colloquialisms or slang, and address others by their proper names or titles unless instructed otherwise. If you're unsure about a particular custom or social nuance, observing the behavior of others can provide subtle guidance.

The art of navigating a formal dinner goes beyond table manners. How you conduct yourself before, during, and after the meal significantly enhances the experience. Before arriving, confirm the dress code to ensure you're appropriately attired. If you're attending a dinner party at someone's private home, aim to arrive about five minutes after the stated time. This brief delay allows the host a little extra time to finalize preparations. Arriving early can fluster the host if everything isn't quite ready. In this context, it's more considerate to be slightly late than to be early. For business meetings, however, punctuality is essential, and arriving five minutes early is considered respectful. Dinner parties, by contrast, follow a more relaxed social rhythm. Upon arrival, greet your host and fellow guests with appropriate salutations and offer a polite handshake, maintaining eye contact. If you're unfamiliar with the seating arrangement, let your host guide you to your designated place.

During the meal, pay attention to its pacing. Don't rush through your food, but don't linger excessively either. Maintain a relaxed and engaging demeanor, and participate in conversation when appropriate. If you choose to decline a particular course or beverage, do so politely and without drawing unnecessary attention to your preference. Any special dietary requirements or strong dislikes should be communicated to your host well in advance, not raised at the table. Whether at a private home or a restaurant, any questions or requests should be addressed quietly to the wait staff or saved for an appropriate moment with the host. Avoid interrupting conversation or drawing attention to yourself unnecessarily.

If you are being hosted in a private home, it's customary to bring a small gift as a token of appreciation. Avoid bringing wine unless you are confident of the host's preferences. A box of quality chocolates or a simple bouquet is often a safe and thoughtful choice. Arriving with a gift shows consideration and respect for the effort your host has made.

Throughout the dinner, thoughtful gestures, such as offering to pour drinks for your neighbors or helping pass dishes, demonstrate social awareness and elevate the dining experience for everyone involved. As the meal concludes, express gratitude to your host for their hospitality. A sincere thank-you note after the event is a considerate gesture of appreciation, especially for formal gatherings or those where significant effort has been put into planning and execution.

Understanding the nuances of formal dining etiquette isn't merely following a strict set of rules. It's about demonstrating respect, consideration, and social awareness, and creating an environment where everyone feels comfortable, valued, and engaged. It's building genuine connections and strengthening relationships through shared experiences. By embracing these principles, formal dinners can transform from potentially intimidating events into opportunities to refine your social graces, foster lasting relationships, and embody the qualities of a true gentleman.

Let's also consider specific situations that may arise during a formal dinner. If you accidentally drop your fork, don't panic. Simply ask the wait staff for a replacement and offer a brief apology only if necessary. The key is handling the situation with grace and minimizing disruption to the meal.

CHAPTER 4

Handling silverware with unfamiliar shapes or sizes may initially seem challenging. If you're unsure, observe fellow diners or discreetly inquire with the wait staff. The key is to maintain a poised demeanor and indicate that you're attentive to the nuances of the dining experience.

Even small actions, like using napkins properly, reflect your awareness of etiquette. Always unfold your napkin before the meal and place it on your lap. Use it to dab your mouth, not to wipe aggressively. If you leave the table temporarily, place your napkin on your chair. At the meal's end, leave the napkin loosely to the left of your plate. These details, while minor, demonstrate refinement and contribute to the overall impression.

Finally, remember that warmth and sincerity always leave a lasting impression. Engage in conversations genuinely, showing interest in others' experiences and opinions. Be attentive to your surroundings, offering assistance when needed, whether by serving food or refilling drinks. These thoughtful gestures speak volumes, transcending the simple adherence to a set of rules. The ultimate goal is to create an atmosphere of ease and cordiality, where meaningful connections are made through shared conversation and mutual respect. Navigating formal dinners isn't about rigidity but more about cultivating a thoughtful, refined approach to social interactions, showcasing your character, and creating an experience that's both memorable and enjoyable.

Creating a Welcoming and Memorable Experience

Hosting, whether for an intimate dinner party or a larger gathering, is a skill that reflects not only social grace but also your consideration and generosity. It's about fostering an atmosphere where everyone feels comfortable, engaged, and valued. The success of any gathering hinges on meticulous planning and thoughtful execution.

The first crucial step is determining the purpose and scale of your event.

Are you hosting a formal dinner party, a casual get-together, a celebratory occasion, or a business networking event? The formality of the event dictates the level of detail required in planning. A formal dinner necessitates a detailed seating plan, a carefully curated menu, and a well-defined dress code, while a casual gathering allows for more relaxed planning. Understanding the event's purpose informs every subsequent decision, from the guest list to the choice of food and drinks.[11]

Crafting the guest list is an art in itself. Consider the dynamics of your guests, ensuring a balanced mix of personalities and interests to foster engaging conversation. Avoid inviting individuals who may clash or create an uncomfortable atmosphere. A carefully curated list fosters a harmonious environment where everyone feels included and comfortable interacting. Once your guest list is finalized, extend invitations well in advance, allowing guests ample time to RSVP. "Include all essential details: date, time, location, dress code (if applicable), and any special instructions.[12]" A well-crafted invitation sets the tone for the event, reflecting your consideration and attention to detail.

The ambiance you create is paramount. Consider the setting. Is your home conducive to the type of event you're planning? If not, explore alternative venues. Lighting plays a critical role in setting the mood. Soft, warm lighting creates a relaxed and intimate atmosphere, while brighter lighting might be suitable for a livelier occasion. Music significantly enhances the atmosphere, creating a background ambiance that fosters conversation without overpowering it. A carefully curated playlist, reflecting the tone of the event, adds a subtle but impactful touch.

Food and drinks are central to any successful gathering. Consider your guests' dietary restrictions and preferences when planning the menu. Offering a variety of choices ensures everyone has something they enjoy. Presentation is crucial; even simple dishes can be elevated with careful plating. For larger events, consider hiring catering services to minimize stress and ensure seamless execution. Drinks should complement the food and occasion. Provide a selection of beverages to cater to diverse tastes, including both alcoholic and non-alcoholic options. Always ensure you have ample ice and appropriate glassware.

The flow of the event is crucial for maintaining a lively and engaging atmosphere. If you're hosting a formal dinner, a well-structured seating plan facilitates conversation. Consider placing individuals with shared interests or complementary personalities together. For larger gatherings, encourage mingling by arranging activities or icebreakers that foster interaction. Engage guests in conversation, showing genuine interest in their lives and experiences. Be attentive to their needs, ensuring everyone feels welcome and included.

As the host, your role extends beyond providing food and drinks. Your presence and demeanor set the tone for the entire event. Be welcoming and approachable, ensuring every guest feels valued and appreciated. Manage the flow of conversation gracefully. Steer it away from potentially contentious topics and facilitate engaging discussions. Pay attention to subtle cues and notice if anyone feels left out or uncomfortable. Your attentiveness and ability to anticipate and address their needs demonstrate your consideration and hospitality.

In business networking events, hosting takes on a slightly different nuance. The objective is not just to create a pleasant atmosphere but also to facilitate meaningful connections. Careful planning is essential, ensuring the event provides ample opportunities for networking. Consider including structured activities or icebreakers to encourage interaction. Provide name tags or a guest list to help attendees connect. As the host, subtly guide and facilitate these interactions, ensuring the event achieves its networking goals.

Beyond logistics, the success of hosting lies in intangible elements: warmth, thoughtfulness, and a genuine desire to make guests feel comfortable and appreciated. Hosting is a form of generosity, a gift of your time, energy, and hospitality. It's about creating an experience that leaves a lasting positive impression, strengthening bonds and fostering meaningful connections. By paying attention to details, anticipating potential challenges, and creating a welcoming atmosphere, you can master the art of hosting and craft memorable events.

Hosting is not just about executing a flawless event. It's about making guests feel seen, heard, and valued by fostering an environment where genuine connections can flourish. While meticulous planning is essential, it's the warmth of your hospitality and the joy you derive from sharing your time with others that truly elevates a gathering from a mere event to an unforgettable experience. The goal is not to impress but to connect, share, and build relationships. This authentic approach, supported by careful planning and execution, ensures you'll be remembered not just for the perfect hors d'oeuvres but for the warmth and hospitality you extended to your guests.

Small, intimate gatherings also benefit from thoughtful planning. A carefully chosen playlist for a quiet evening with close friends, a thoughtfully prepared meal for a family dinner, or the simple act of offering a guest a comfortable chair and a refreshing drink. These small acts of hospitality collectively create a welcoming environment. Successful hosting is about attention to detail and a sincere desire to make others feel welcome and appreciated, regardless of the event's scale.

Consider the value of pre-event communication. A brief follow-up email a few days before the event, reminding guests of the details and reiterating your enthusiasm, enhances the overall experience. It shows you care and helps prevent last-minute confusion. This added touch demonstrates your thoughtfulness and commitment to creating a seamless and enjoyable event for everyone.

CHAPTER 4

Mastering the art of hosting is a continuous process of learning and refinement. Each event presents an opportunity to adapt and enhance your skills. Don't be afraid to experiment, try new ideas, and incorporate your personal style. The most successful hosts are genuine, adaptable, and committed to creating an enjoyable experience for their guests. The key is to cultivate an environment where meaningful connections and positive interactions thrive. Ultimately, the true measure of your success as a host isn't flawless execution but the lasting, positive memories you create for yourself and your guests. It's the warmth and authentic connection that make an event truly memorable.

Thoughtfulness and Consideration

The art of gift-giving, often overlooked, is a powerful expression of thoughtfulness and consideration, significantly impacting personal and professional relationships. It's far more than simply purchasing an item. It's a carefully curated gesture that reflects your understanding of the recipient and the occasion. A well-chosen gift demonstrates respect, appreciation, and a genuine connection. Conversely, an ill-conceived gift can inadvertently communicate insensitivity or a lack of consideration, potentially damaging a relationship. Therefore, mastering the nuances of gift-giving etiquette is crucial for navigating social and professional landscapes with grace and refinement.

Understanding the context is the first crucial element. The occasion dictates the appropriate level of formality and the type of gift. A small, thoughtful token might suffice for a casual acquaintance's birthday, whereas a more substantial and carefully selected present is expected for significant life events such as a wedding or a milestone birthday. For professional colleagues, gifts should always maintain a level of decorum, avoiding anything that could be interpreted as overly personal or inappropriate. A corporate gift, for example, should enhance the work environment or reflect the company's values.

Consideration of the recipient's personality, preferences, and lifestyle is paramount. A gift reflecting their hobbies, interests, or aspirations demonstrates a genuine understanding and appreciation of who they are. This requires thoughtful observation and perhaps even discreet inquiry. For instance, noticing a colleague consistently admiring a particular artist's work might inspire you to gift a catalogue of their latest exhibition. Conversely, gifting something generic or based solely on your own preferences suggests a lack of consideration.

The presentation of the gift is equally important. The manner in which you give a gift speaks volumes. Avoid simply handing it over; take a moment to express your sentiments and the reason behind your choice. A handwritten card expressing your appreciation and well wishes adds a personal touch that elevates the gift. Avoid overly effusive or insincere language, opting for sincerity and genuine feeling. Furthermore, the presentation should align with the occasion and relationship. A formally wrapped present with a ribbon is appropriate for formal occasions, while a more casual presentation might be suitable for close friends or family.

The monetary value of the gift is less important than the thought behind it. It's not about the price tag but the intention. An inexpensive yet carefully chosen and personalized gift can be far more meaningful than an expensive, impersonal item. Indeed, overspending can even be perceived negatively, suggesting a desire to impress rather than convey genuine affection or appreciation. The focus should always be on choosing something appropriate that reflects your relationship with the recipient.

Navigating the complexities of gift-giving in the professional sphere demands particular attention to detail. Corporate gift-giving has specific protocols, often dictated by company policy and ethical considerations. Gifts should never be offered in exchange for favors or to influence decisions. Transparency and a clear understanding of ethical guidelines are vital to avoid any perception of impropriety or conflict of interest. Instead, corporate gifts should aim to enhance relationships, strengthen professional networks, and show appreciation for achievements or collaborations.

When choosing a gift for a professional colleague, opt for something tasteful and practical. Items related to their work, such as a high-quality pen or a personalized stationery set, can be appropriate. Alternatively, a gift that reflects shared interests outside of work can strengthen the bond. However, always maintain professional distance, ensuring the gift does not cross boundaries of appropriateness. Avoid overly personal items or gifts that might be considered too intimate for a professional setting. Similarly, gifts associated with religious holidays or personal beliefs should be approached with caution, considering the recipient's background and potential sensitivities.

Furthermore, cultural nuances should be considered when choosing a gift for someone from a different background. Certain gifts may hold symbolic meaning or be considered inappropriate in other cultures. Conducting prior research ensures your gift is well-received and culturally sensitive, showing respect and avoiding unintended offense. Understanding cultural customs regarding gift-giving, such as the appropriate time to give a gift, the manner of presentation, and the significance of certain colors or symbols, enhances the overall experience and prevents misunderstandings.

The art of gift-giving involves a multifaceted approach. It necessitates careful consideration of the occasion, the recipient's preferences, and your relationship with them. The emphasis should always be on thoughtfulness, sincerity, and genuine appreciation. While the monetary value of a gift is secondary, the time and effort invested in selecting a thoughtful present speak volumes. Mastering this art enhances not only your social interactions but also your ability to build and nurture meaningful relationships in both personal and professional realms. It's a skill that reflects empathy, understanding, and refinement, which are becoming traits of a truly cultivated gentleman. The act of giving, when approached with thoughtfulness and sincerity, strengthens bonds and fosters goodwill, embodying the essence of grace and refinement in social interactions. A well-chosen gift is not just an object; it's a statement of your consideration and respect. It encourages connection and leaves a lasting impression. This mindful approach elevates gift-giving from a mere formality to a meaningful expression of appreciation.

Understanding the recipient's lifestyle is equally crucial. Are they a minimalist who appreciates experiences over possessions? In that case, a gift certificate for a massage or a weekend getaway might be far more appropriate than a material item. Are they avid collectors with a passion for specific items? A carefully researched addition to their collection demonstrates a genuine understanding of their interests. This detailed consideration underscores the importance of moving beyond generic gift choices and engaging in thoughtful reflection, which demonstrates a deep understanding and strengthens the connection between you and the recipient.

The timing of gift-giving is another subtle yet significant element of etiquette. A birthday present should ideally be given on or around the actual date. Similarly, holiday gifts should be presented during the relevant season. However, situations may arise where timing is flexible. In such instances, a prompt and heartfelt explanation for the delay mitigates any potential awkwardness. This adaptability and conscientiousness reflects awareness of social nuances and a commitment to gracious interactions. Likewise, presenting a gift too early or too late can subtly alter the perceived value and significance of the gesture.

Beyond tangible items, the most valuable gifts often involve acts of service or shared experiences. Offering your time, assistance, or companionship can be incredibly meaningful, especially for individuals who prioritize experiences over material possessions. A thoughtful gesture such as offering to help with a chore, providing support during a challenging period, or planning a special outing demonstrates a deeper level of care and consideration than a material gift. These acts of service, when genuine, show commitment to the relationship and create lasting positive memories.

Ultimately, the etiquette surrounding gift-giving is a delicate dance of consideration and sincerity. It's an art that requires careful observation, thoughtful reflection, and a genuine desire to connect with the recipient on a deeper level. Choosing and giving a gift is not merely a transaction; it's an opportunity to express appreciation, foster stronger relationships, and leave a lasting positive impression. By embracing thoughtfulness, consideration, and cultural awareness, you can elevate this simple act to a sophisticated expression of refined sensibilities. A well-chosen and gracefully presented gift has a far-reaching impact, leaving a positive imprint on the recipient and reinforcing the enduring significance of interpersonal connections.

Engaging with Diverse Groups

The ability to engage in meaningful conversations with diverse groups of people is a cornerstone of social grace and sophistication. It's a skill honed through practice, observation, and a genuine interest in others. This extends beyond small talk. It involves active listening, empathy, and respect for different perspectives and backgrounds. In today's interconnected world, mastering this art is not just a social advantage but a necessity for building strong personal and professional relationships.

One crucial aspect is understanding the dynamics of group conversations. Avoid dominating the discussion; instead, strive for a balanced exchange of ideas. Actively listen to what others are saying, and pay attention not just to words but also to the nonverbal cues, such as body language, tone of voice, and facial expressions. This attentiveness demonstrates respect and fosters a sense of connection. When it's your turn to speak, be mindful of your tone and delivery, ensuring you are respectful and engaging.

Furthermore, adapting your communication style to different individuals is paramount. People communicate in varied ways, influenced by their cultural backgrounds, personalities, and experiences. What is acceptable in one setting may be inappropriate in another. Observing the social cues within a group is essential. Are people generally reserved or outgoing? Formal or informal? Understanding this context allows you to adjust your approach, accordingly, preventing misunderstandings or unintentional offense.

For example, in a formal business setting, discussing professional topics and maintaining appropriate personal space is expected. Conversely, in a casual social setting, a more relaxed and informal approach may be better received. The key lies in observing the nuances of social interaction and adapting accordingly. This adaptability showcases not only social intelligence but also a deep respect for those involved.

Navigating conversations with individuals from different cultural backgrounds requires an extra layer of sensitivity. Cultural norms significantly influence communication styles. Directness, for instance, is valued in some cultures but considered rude in others. Similarly, personal space, eye contact, and hand gestures can have different interpretations across cultures. Before engaging in conversation with someone from a different background, it's beneficial to familiarize yourself with common cultural norms and etiquette. This is not about memorizing a checklist but rather cultivating an open mind and a willingness to learn.

A mindful, respectful, and observant approach is best. If you are unsure about something, err on the side of caution. Asking polite questions and showing genuine interest in someone's culture is often welcomed. Frame these inquiries as a way to understand and appreciate their perspective rather than as judgment or critique. The goal is to build bridges of understanding, not walls of misunderstanding.

Another crucial skill is active listening. This goes beyond hearing words.[13] It's about truly understanding another's perspective. Pay close attention to their words, tone, and body language. "Ask clarifying questions to ensure you understand their message correctly.[14"] Summarize their points to demonstrate that you have been listening attentively. When someone feels heard and understood, they are more likely to engage in a meaningful and productive conversation. Active listening is not only a sign of respect but also a powerful tool for building rapport and trust.

Additionally, be mindful of your own biases and assumptions. We all have preconceived notions, but recognizing and challenging them is essential. Approach each conversation with an open mind, willing to learn from those with different perspectives. This willingness to engage with diverse viewpoints is a hallmark of intellectual curiosity and a crucial aspect of social sophistication.

In business settings, this skill is especially critical. Working in diverse teams is increasingly the norm, and the ability to communicate effectively across cultural and personality differences is paramount for success. Effective teamwork requires not only the ability to share ideas clearly but also to appreciate the perspectives of colleagues. Your communication style should always reflect respect and consideration for others, irrespective of seniority or position. A respectful and understanding approach fosters a more collaborative and productive work environment.

Beyond the workplace, engaging meaningfully with diverse groups enhances one's personal life. Whether at a social gathering, a family event, or a community meeting, the ability to converse respectfully strengthens connections. This skillset also extends to online interactions. The internet is a global platform, and maintaining courteous and respectful communication across digital platforms is essential. Whether through emails, social media, or forums, your virtual interactions should reflect the same level of respect and consideration as face-to-face conversations.

Finally, genuine interest is the foundation of successful social interactions. Approach each conversation with a desire to learn and connect. Ask open-ended questions that encourage others to share their thoughts and experiences. Show empathy and understanding, even when you do not agree with their perspective. By focusing on genuine connection rather than superficial pleasantries, you will build stronger, more meaningful relationships. This approach reflects not just social graces but also genuine human connection, which are hallmarks of a refined gentleman.

The ability to engage thoughtfully and respectfully with diverse groups is not just a social skill; it's a testament to personal growth, intellectual curiosity, and respect for the human experience. It's a skill that will serve you well throughout your life, enriching both personal and professional spheres. Mastering this art demonstrates both social awareness and emotional intelligence, qualities that hold lasting value in modern life.

Investing in these skills yields rewards in richer relationships and greater understanding of the world. The effort required is undoubtedly worthwhile, leading to a more fulfilling and meaningful life. By practicing these techniques, you can cultivate a genuine ability to connect with people from all walks of life, fostering strong relationships and enriching your own life in the process. This is the essence of social sophistication, a seamless blend of traditional grace and modern understanding.

Chapter 5

Personal Style – Cultivating a Refined Image

Timeless Elegance

Building a capsule wardrobe isn't about deprivation; it's about strategic curation. It's the process of identifying core pieces that work harmoniously together, which maximize versatility and minimize decision fatigue. It's a collection of carefully curated, interchangeable items of clothing that maximize how many outfits you own. This approach goes beyond fleeting trends, focusing instead on timeless elegance and lasting quality. The goal isn't to own less but to own better pieces that serve multiple purposes and reflect a refined personal style. Think of it as an investment in yourself, demonstrating not just an eye for aesthetics but an appreciation for quality and sustainability.

A successful capsule wardrobe starts with understanding your lifestyle and personal preferences. What are your typical daily activities? What kind of social and professional events do you attend? What colors and styles suit you best? Honest self-assessment is crucial. Begin by evaluating your current wardrobe, identifying the pieces you wear most often and those that consistently earn compliments. These serve as the foundation of your capsule collection. Remove or donate items that are damaged, ill-fitting, or no longer align with your style.

Once you've streamlined your closet, you can begin building your core collection with versatile garments that mix and match effortlessly. For the modern gentleman, this might include:

- **Suits:** At least one well-tailored suit in navy or charcoal is essential. This serves as the cornerstone of professional attire and can adapt to various formal occasions. A lighter suit, such as light gray or beige, is a useful addition for warmer months or more relaxed settings.
- **Tuxedos:** Every gentleman should own a classic black tuxedo. While it may not be worn often, having a well-tailored tuxedo ready ensures you are properly dressed when a formal event arises. Choose a single-breasted style with a satin or grosgrain lapel, and pair it with a formal white shirt, black bow tie, and polished black shoes. Simplicity and fit are key. A tuxedo is not just about looking elegant, it shows respect for the formality of the occasion.
- **Blazers:** A navy blazer is incredibly versatile, pairing well with chinos for a smart-casual look, dress pants for formal occasions, or even jeans for a polished weekend outfit. A brown or patterned blazer can further expand your wardrobe options.
- **Dress Pants:** A few pairs of well-fitted dress pants in neutral shades like navy, charcoal, and black are essential. Wool or wool blends provide durability and a refined appearance.
- **Chinos:** A sophisticated yet relaxed alternative to dress pants. Opt for classic colors like navy, khaki, or olive.
- **Shirts:** A selection of crisp, well-fitting shirts in solid colors, such as white, light blue, and gray, forms the backbone of a wardrobe. Introduce subtle stripes or patterns for variety, including both long- and short-sleeved options.
- **T-shirts:** High-quality, neutral-colored t-shirts (white, navy, gray, black)

are ideal for layering or casual wear. Prioritize well-made, durable fabrics.
- **Sweaters:** A versatile mix of sweaters, including a classic crew neck, V-neck, and perhaps a cardigan, adds warmth and texture. Stick to timeless hues like navy, gray, and camel.
- **Outerwear:** A classic trench coat, a refined overcoat, or a high-quality leather jacket enhances both style and functionality. Choose a piece that complements your wardrobe and fits well.
- **Shoes:** A well-rounded shoe collection is essential. This might include dress shoes (oxfords or loafers), casual options (boat shoes or driving shoes), and a quality pair of boots. Shoe quality significantly impacts the overall look of an outfit.
- **Accessories:** Thoughtfully chosen accessories elevate an outfit. A well-made tie, pocket square, belt, and stylish watch add refinement. Ensure accessories complement both your personal style and the occasion.

Beyond individual pieces, material quality is key. Investing in durable, well-made items crafted from wool, cotton, linen, and leather, ensures both longevity and style. These fabrics not only age well but also enhance the overall look of your wardrobe. Proper tailoring is equally important. Even the finest garments look better when they fit perfectly, so consider professional alterations for a polished finish.

Building a capsule wardrobe is a gradual process. It requires careful thought, experimentation, and a strong sense of personal style. Start with the essentials, then gradually introduce pieces that complement your collection. As you wear your wardrobe, you'll refine your preferences and adjust accordingly.

Context matters. A capsule wardrobe for a city-based professional will differ from one suited to an outdoor lifestyle. A lawyer's wardrobe, for instance, will emphasize tailored suits and crisp shirts, while a creative director might incorporate textured fabrics and bolder colors. The key is adapting these principles to your unique needs.

The true beauty of a capsule wardrobe lies in its simplicity and efficiency. It allows you to dress well without the stress of constant decision-making. By reducing clutter and prioritizing sustainability, you free up mental energy for more important things. Thoughtfully selecting high-quality, timeless pieces results in a wardrobe that's not only stylish but also a reflection of personal refinement.

Timeless elegance is the guiding principle. Avoid fleeting trends in favor of classic styles and neutral colors that remain relevant for years. A well-chosen navy blazer, for example, never goes out of style and pairs effortlessly with countless outfits.

Beyond the clothing itself, proper garment care is essential. Cleaning and storing pieces correctly significantly extends their lifespan. Learn to care for different fabrics, and invest in quality hangers and storage solutions to maintain their condition.

Finally, remember that a capsule wardrobe is a journey, not a destination. It evolves with your lifestyle and preferences over time. As your style matures, you can refine your collection, ensuring it remains both functional and reflective of your taste. This approach offers flexibility, adaptability, and ongoing refinement. In the end, a well-curated wardrobe isn't just about clothing but it's an investment in your image and, by extension, yourself.

Enhancing your Appearance

Understanding the nuances of fit and tailoring is essential in elevating personal style. It's not just about wearing clothes. You need to wear them well. A perfectly tailored garment transforms the wearer, instilling confidence and sophistication that goes beyond mere aesthetics. It reflects attention to detail, an appreciation for quality craftsmanship, and a commitment to presenting oneself at their best. This extends beyond appearance. It's about feeling comfortable in your own skin, which in turn influences how you engage with the world.

The importance of proper fit cannot be overstated. Ill-fitting clothing, no matter the price or brand, can undermine even the most carefully curated wardrobe. A suit that's too tight restricts movement, creating an uncomfortable and unprofessional impression. On the other hand, a suit that's too loose appears sloppy, and diminishes authority and credibility. This principle applies to all garments, from shirts and trousers to outerwear and accessories. A shirt with sleeves that are too long or short, a jacket that hangs awkwardly, or trousers that bunch at the ankles all contribute to a less-than-polished look. Mastering fit means striking a balance, such as clothes that are neither too tight or too loose, and allow for ease of movement while maintaining a clean, structured silhouette.

Tailoring, the pinnacle of refined style, takes fit to another level. It's the process of modifying garments to achieve a precise, personalized fit. A skilled tailor can adjust seams, shorten sleeves, taper trousers, and make subtle alterations that allow clothing to drape perfectly on the body. These details transform garments from simple coverings into flattering, form-enhancing pieces. A tailored suit, for example, appears sharper and more structured than its off-the-rack counterpart. The difference is subtle but profound, signaling an understanding of sartorial elegance and a discerning eye for detail.

Investing in tailoring is investing in oneself. It acknowledges that clothing is more than a commodity but it's an integral part of personal presentation. While the cost of tailoring varies based on the complexity of alterations and the skill of the tailor, the return on investment is immeasurable. A well-tailored garment doesn't just look better; it feels better. It enhances posture, encourages confident body language, and promotes a heightened sense of self-assurance. The impact extends beyond the individual, shaping how others perceive and respond to you in professional and social settings.

Choosing the right tailor is crucial. Look for someone with a strong reputation and proven experience. Personal recommendations from colleagues or friends can be invaluable. Don't hesitate to visit multiple tailors before making a decision. Assess their workspace, examine their craftsmanship, and discuss your needs. A skilled tailor will take the time to understand your body type, style preferences, and the function of each garment. They will offer expert guidance to ensure a perfect fit, elevating your wardrobe from ordinary to exceptional. This collaboration between client and tailor is essential because it's a partnership in refining a sophisticated, polished image.

Tailoring isn't just for suits. A well-fitted shirt, for instance, should sit smoothly across the shoulders and chest, with sleeves ending precisely at the wrist. The collar should lay comfortably against the neck, neither too tight nor too loose. Likewise, trousers should fall neatly without excessive bunching at the waist or ankles. Even small details, such as jacket sleeve length or button placement, can significantly impact the overall impression. These refinements may seem minor, but together, they create a cohesive, polished aesthetic.

The benefits of understanding fit and tailoring extend beyond professional settings. In social environments, a polished appearance influences interactions and first impressions. A refined image conveys self-respect and confidence, fostering trust and credibility. Whether attending a formal event, a casual gathering, or a business function, attention to fit and tailoring demonstrates both personal pride and respect for the occasion. It's a subtle yet powerful way of projecting confidence and reinforcing your personal brand.

Fabric selection also plays a role. The drape of a garment affects its overall fit and appearance. Heavier fabrics, such as wool, behave differently than

CHAPTER 5

lighter ones like linen. Understanding these distinctions is essential when choosing garments and making tailoring decisions. Additionally, how a fabric responds to alterations can impact the final outcome. An experienced tailor considers these factors, ensuring that adjustments maintain both the garment's integrity and aesthetic appeal.

The tailoring process itself is an educational experience. Observing a tailor at work offers deeper insight into garment construction and fit. This knowledge proves invaluable when selecting clothing in the future, enabling more informed purchases and minimizing the need for major alterations. It's a journey of refinement, an opportunity to appreciate craftsmanship and understand how clothing enhances personal presentation.

Fit and tailoring aren't static concepts. As one's body changes, so should one's approach to clothing. Periodic adjustments may be necessary to maintain a sharp silhouette, not as a sign of failure but as a reflection of ongoing self-improvement. A refined image is an evolving pursuit, and mastering fit is a key component of achieving and maintaining that polished, sophisticated aesthetic.

An investment in fit and tailoring yields lasting rewards, both professionally and personally. The confidence that comes from wearing well-fitting, expertly tailored garments is invaluable. It shapes how you perceive yourself and how others perceive you. It's a silent yet powerful statement of self-respect, attention to detail, and appreciation for quality, which are hallmarks of a true gentleman.

Adding Personality and Refinement

Accessorizing is the art of subtle enhancement; the final flourish that elevates an ensemble from merely adequate to truly memorable. It adds personality, injects individual flair, and demonstrates a keen eye for detail. While a perfectly tailored suit or an impeccably chosen shirt forms the foundation of a refined image, accessories orchestrate the symphony of personal style. They serve as silent storytellers, revealing nuances of character and taste that words often fail to capture. Understanding how to use accessories effectively is crucial for any gentleman seeking to cultivate a polished and sophisticated appearance.

The Power of Restraint
The key to successful accessorizing lies in restraint. Overdoing it's a common pitfall that can create a cluttered look and detract from the overall impression. The goal is to select pieces that enhance an outfit without overwhelming it. Quality should always take precedence over quantity. A single, well-chosen accessory, such as a meticulously crafted watch or a luxurious silk tie, has far more impact than a collection of inexpensive, poorly made items.

Context Matters
Accessories should always be chosen with the occasion in mind. What works for a business meeting differs from what suits a weekend outing or a formal dinner. In professional settings, a high-quality leather briefcase, a simple yet elegant watch, and perhaps a discreet tie bar are ideal choices. More playful, expressive accessories, such as a colorful pocket square, a stylish bracelet, or distinctive cufflinks, are better suited for casual or social occasions.

Let's explore key accessories and their role in refining personal style:

- **Watches: A Statement of Sophistication:** A watch is more than a timepiece; it's a reflection of personal style and an appreciation for craftsmanship. A classic leather-strap watch with a clean, uncluttered face is a timeless choice that suits nearly any occasion. For business settings, opt for a subdued design, while more intricate or embellished pieces can be reserved for leisure. Regardless of style, maintenance is essential. A scratched crystal or loose strap can instantly diminish an otherwise refined impression. Knowledge of a watch's history and craftsmanship can also spark engaging conversations.

- **Ties and Pocket Squares: Subtle Elegance:** Ties and pocket squares are cornerstones of masculine elegance, offering opportunities for self-expression within the framework of formal dress:
- The tie, often the focal point of a suit, should complement the shirt and jacket without clashing. Subtle patterns and muted tones work best in professional settings, while bolder colors and intricate designs may be suitable for relaxed occasions.
- The pocket square adds a subtle yet distinctive touch. It should contrast with the tie rather than match it exactly; just think of a complementary palette or a slight variation in texture. Mastering different folding techniques allows for greater creativity and refinement. The art of selecting and pairing ties and pocket squares is a journey of discovery, an opportunity to refine personal style over time.
- **Cufflinks and Tie Bars: Small Details, Big Impact:** These understated accessories contribute significantly to a polished appearance:
- High-quality cufflinks elevate a French-cuffed shirt, exuding sophistication. Simple, elegant designs are best for professional settings, while more elaborate styles can be worn on less formal occasions.
- A well-chosen tie bar keeps a tie in place, ensuring a sharp, composed look. It should be proportional to the tie's width, neither too large nor too small, to maintain balance.
- **Belts and Shoes: The Foundation of a Well-Dressed Man:** Though often overlooked, belts and shoes are fundamental accessories that can make or break an outfit.
- A high-quality leather belt, matching the color of one's shoes, adds a refined touch. The buckle should be understated, and proportionate. Oversized or flashy buckles are best avoided in professional settings.
- Shoes, perhaps the most visible accessory, significantly influence overall presentation. Well-maintained, polished leather or suede shoes signal attention to detail and a commitment to refinement. Their style should align with the occasion, seamlessly complementing the rest of the outfit. Investing in high-quality footwear and keeping it in pristine condition is a testament to personal pride and sophistication.

- **Jewelry: Less is More:** Men's jewelry should be approached with discretion. A classic wristwatch and a wedding band are often sufficient. If opting for additional pieces, such as a bracelet or necklace, ensure they are understated and work harmoniously with the outfit. Excessive layering or overly flashy designs can appear distracting rather than refined. The focus should always be on subtlety and elegance rather than ostentation.
- **Briefcases and Bags: Functional Elegance:** The right bag speaks volumes about a man's professionalism and style. A high-quality leather briefcase is a staple for business settings, while a refined messenger bag or tote may be more appropriate for casual occasions. Regardless of style, a bag should always be in excellent condition, since scuffed, worn-out leather can undermine an otherwise polished image.
- **Additional Accessories:** Other accessories, such as scarves, sunglasses, and hats, should be chosen with the same attention to detail. A well-chosen scarf adds warmth and sophistication in colder months, while high-quality sunglasses offer both protection and a sleek aesthetic. Hats, when worn appropriately, can be a stylish finishing touch, though they require careful consideration to avoid appearing outdated or out of place.

The Importance of Maintenance

Beyond selection, proper care of accessories is essential. Leather goods require regular conditioning to maintain their integrity, while shoes should be polished and stored properly.

Watches should be serviced periodically, and keep metal accessories should free of tarnish. Taking care of accessories reflects not only a commitment to quality but also a meticulous approach to personal presentation.

A Journey of Refinement

Accessorizing is a personal journey, one that evolves through experimentation and experience. Trying different combinations, observing what works, and refining choices over time are all part of developing a unique, sophisticated style. However, restraint and context should always guide decisions. Accessories should enhance an overall look, never detract from it.

By thoughtfully selecting and wearing accessories, a man can elevate his presence, leaving a lasting impression that speaks of confidence, refinement, and attention to detail. It's these subtle touches that transform an outfit from ordinary to exceptional, underscoring the art of true elegance.

Maintaining a Polished Look

Grooming is not merely a matter of aesthetics; it's a discipline, a reflection of self-respect, and a statement of intent. It signifies a commitment to personal excellence, a silent yet powerful indicator of one's attention to detail. A man's presence is not solely defined by what he wears but by how he carries himself, and grooming plays an indispensable role in shaping that perception. A well-tailored suit loses its impact when accompanied by unkempt hair or an unshaven face. True refinement is holistic, an orchestration of every detail that contributes to an overall impression of competence, confidence, and poise.

Cleanliness is the foundation upon which grooming is built. Daily showering is not simply about washing away sweat and impurities; it's a ritual of renewal, preparing both body and mind for the day ahead. The choice of cleanser matters, harsh soaps can strip the skin, leaving it dry and irritated, while the right body wash can cleanse gently while maintaining the skin's natural balance. A man should know his skin type, just as he knows his wardrobe because what works for one may not suit another. Exfoliation, performed once or twice a week, removes dead skin cells, promoting a smoother, healthier appearance. Hydration follows naturally; a quality moisturizer ensures skin remains supple and resilient, especially after shaving or exposure to harsh environments.

Hair, often the most immediately noticeable aspect of grooming, demands equal attention. A haircut is not just about neatness, but it's a signature of personal style. The right cut should complement both face shape and lifestyle, striking the right balance between professional polish and individual expression. Maintenance is key; even the most well-chosen style falters if left unattended. Hair should be washed regularly, but not excessively, as natural oils are essential for health and shine. For those experiencing thinning, subtle adjustments in styling can create the illusion of volume.

Facial hair requires conscious upkeep, whether one opts for a clean shave or a carefully maintained beard. A beard should be trimmed, shaped, and kept free of stray hairs, a subtle refinement that separates a well-groomed man from one who merely lets his facial hair grow unchecked. Washing a beard is as essential as washing the hair on one's head, preventing buildup and ensuring a fresh appearance. The clean-shaven look demands its own discipline, especially regular shaving. Sharp razors and proper technique prevent irritation, ingrown hairs, and uneven results. A quality shaving cream, a proper razor, and an aftershave balm are small but significant investments in comfort and presentation.

Hands, often overlooked, are a direct reflection of a man's approach to detail. They are visible in nearly every social and professional interaction, whether shaking hands, signing a document, or gesturing during conversation. Rough, unkempt hands or uneven, dirty nails suggest carelessness, undermining an otherwise polished presentation. Keeping nails trimmed, clean, and smooth is not an indulgence; it's a mark of self-respect. While few men will opt for a professional manicure, regular maintenance ensures that hands remain well-groomed, soft, and presentable.

Oral hygiene is non-negotiable. No amount of refined dress or eloquence can compensate for neglected teeth or bad breath. Brushing and flossing twice daily should be second nature, along with regular visits to the dentist for cleaning and checkups. Fresh breath is as essential as a pressed shirt. Strong odors, whether from poor hygiene or dietary choices, can be distracting at best and off-putting at worst. A discreet use of mouthwash or breath mints is a wise precaution, particularly in professional and social settings where first impressions matter.

Scent, when wielded correctly, is one of the most powerful yet understated elements of a man's presence. A carefully chosen fragrance should be an extension of personality: subtle, refined, and never overwhelming. Too much cologne can be more detrimental than none at all. A light application to pulse points, such as the wrists and collarbone, ensures a scent that is noticeable only in close proximity, never imposing on others. The right fragrance depends on the setting. Clean, fresh scents work well for daytime and professional environments, while deeper, more complex notes are better suited for evening affairs. Regardless of preference, the goal remains the same: to leave an impression that is inviting rather than overpowering.

Even the feet, often hidden from view, demand attention. Neglect here is not only a matter of appearance but of comfort and well-being. Regular washing, the occasional use of foot powder to control moisture, and well-fitted, breathable shoes prevent common issues such as odor or discomfort. Toenails, though easily ignored, should be trimmed and maintained with the same care as fingernails. A man who takes care of his feet is a man who understands that true refinement is not selective, but it extends to every aspect of self-presentation, even those that are not immediately visible.

Beyond hygiene and grooming lies an understanding of how one's physical attributes interact with clothing. Fit is paramount; even the most luxurious fabrics lose their elegance if the proportions are off. A suit should frame the body correctly, emphasizing strengths while downplaying weaknesses. Shirts should rest smoothly on the shoulders, sleeves falling to the proper length, while trousers should break just enough over polished shoes. Regardless of formality, neatness is essential because wrinkled, ill-fitting garments can undo the impact of even the most dedicated grooming routine.

Consistency is the unspoken rule that ties all these elements together. Grooming is not a one-time effort but a habit, a discipline maintained day after day. It requires attentiveness, an understanding that small lapses accumulate, gradually shaping how one is perceived. The man who commits to these details signals more than just personal pride because he communicates reliability, professionalism, and self-discipline.

But beyond outward appearance, there is a deeper principle at play. Good grooming is not about vanity; it's about respect. Respect for oneself, for the people one encounters, and for the opportunities that arise when one presents the best version of himself to the world. The man who understands this does not see grooming as a chore, but as a daily ritual of self-care, mostly as an investment that yields confidence, credibility, and an undeniable presence.

Adapting your Style

The foundation of a polished image lies not only in meticulous grooming but also in an acute understanding of appropriate attire. Dressing for different occasions transcends the simple act of choosing clothes. It's an art form that communicates respect, awareness, and a keen grasp of social cues. It's about harmonizing your style with appropriate context, reflecting both your personality and your ability to adapt to the nuances of the setting. This goes beyond owning a well-stocked wardrobe because it demands discernment and the capacity to align your personal style with diverse environments.

Consider the business world. While a power suit is a timeless choice, it may not suit every professional occasion. A high-stakes board meeting calls for a formal look; perhaps a dark suit, a crisp shirt, and a conservative tie crafted from quality fabric. Loud patterns and flashy accessories should be avoided; understated elegance speaks volumes. The aim is to exude competence and professionalism without detracting from the business at hand. By contrast, a casual business environment, such as a team lunch or a relaxed meeting, permits more flexibility. A tailored blazer paired with chinos and a button-down shirt achieves a polished yet approachable look, and maintains the standards of professional presentation.

Social settings demand a distinct approach. For instance, a formal dinner party may require a tuxedo or dark suit, depending on the host's expectations. In these instances, the focus shifts from rigid professionalism to sophisticated elegance. Accessories like cufflinks or a pocket square add personal flair without overwhelming the outfit. At a casual barbecue or picnic, opt for attire that balances comfort and style. Chinos paired with a polo or linen shirt can strike the perfect tone. The goal is to project an effortless yet refined demeanor.

Different occasions call for tailored considerations. A wedding, for instance, necessitates careful adherence to the invitation's level of formality. A black-tie event demands a tuxedo, while a less formal ceremony may permit a dark suit or a stylish sports jacket with well-chosen trousers. Seasonal and daytime variations also influence choices. A summer wedding warrants lighter fabrics and brighter tones, whereas a winter affair benefits from richer colors and heavier materials.

Sporting events are another scenario where thoughtful attire is key. Comfort is essential, but an outfit can remain stylish and polished without veering into excessive casualness. Well-fitted jeans paired with a sweater or jacket and clean, comfortable shoes can project understated sophistication. Even informal gatherings benefit from a degree of care in presentation.

Dressing appropriately also entails cultural sensitivity. Attire suitable in one culture may not translate well in another. Researching the customs and norms of a specific culture is essential when attending social or professional international events. Demonstrating cultural awareness fosters positive relationships and minimizes the risk of misunderstandings.

Mastering the art of dressing for any occasion begins with an appreciation for the unspoken cues of each setting. Consider the dress code, the event's location, and its overall tone. When uncertain, it's better to err on the side of formality, especially in professional contexts, where a polished appearance underscores respect and competence.

Building a versatile wardrobe is integral to this process. Investing in high-quality, adaptable pieces, such as a tailored suit, crisp shirts, versatile jackets, and a selection of ties, creates a solid foundation. These elements can be mixed and matched to suit a variety of occasions. Elevate your wardrobe further with carefully chosen accessories, such as high-quality shoes, belts, and watches, which add subtle refinement.

Accessories enhance your outfit and express individuality when chosen thoughtfully. A pocket square or a tasteful tie can elevate a suit for a business meeting or formal event. Similarly, a sophisticated watch adds understated elegance. Jewelry should remain simple and tasteful, complementing your look without overpowering it. The goal is to enhance, not overshadow, the overall presentation.

Equally important is ensuring a proper fit. Ill-fitting clothes, no matter how stylish or expensive, undermine your appearance. Investing in tailoring ensures that each garment complements your physique and conveys attention to detail, a hallmark of polished style.

Maintaining your wardrobe is as critical as building it. Regular cleaning, pressing, and appropriate storage preserve the longevity and quality of your clothes, ensuring they look impeccable. Shoes, too, require care. Well-maintained footwear adds a crucial element of sophistication to any outfit. Such diligence reflects respect for yourself and others while reinforcing your image as polished and capable.

Dressing appropriately involves more than simply choosing clothes; it's an ongoing commitment to refinement, adaptability, and awareness. It's a medium for expressing personal style while respecting the context and setting. By cultivating this skill, you project a confident, professional image that resonates positively in both business and social spheres. This thoughtful approach underscores your self-respect and consideration for others, and creates lasting impressions and fosters meaningful connections. Ultimately, dressing well is not about rigid conformity but about communicating effectively, paving the way for success.

Chapter 6

The Art of Appreciation – Wine, Spirits and Cigars

Understanding the Basics

Wine appreciation, for the modern gentleman, transcends mere imbibing. It's an exploration of history, geography, and artistry, all culminating in a sensory experience. This journey begins with understanding the basics—a foundation upon which you can build a sophisticated palate and confident conversational skills related to this refined pursuit.

Firstly, let's address the grape. The world of wine is vast and varied, largely shaped by the grape varietal itself. Cabernet Sauvignon, for instance, known for its bold tannins and full body, often hails from warmer climates like Bordeaux, France, or Napa Valley, California. Its structured nature makes it an ideal companion to hearty red meats and aged cheeses. Conversely, Pinot Noir, a delicate and nuanced grape, thrives in cooler regions such as Burgundy, France, or Oregon's Willamette Valley. Its lighter body and earthy notes pair beautifully with salmon, roasted chicken, and mushrooms.

Understanding the inherent characteristics of different grape varietals, such as their acidity, tannin levels, and flavor profiles—is crucial to appreciating their individual merits. This knowledge allows you to choose wines that complement specific meals and occasions. Consider exploring regions known for particular varietals. Learning about the terroir—the soil, climate, and other environmental factors—further enriches your understanding and appreciation. A bottle of Barolo from Piedmont, Italy, made from Nebbiolo grapes, will differ significantly from a Napa Valley Cabernet Sauvignon, not only due to terroir but also because of the fundamental differences between the grape varietals themselves.

Beyond the grape, the winemaking process itself heavily influences the final product. From the methods of harvesting and crushing to fermentation techniques and aging in oak barrels, each step contributes to the wine's unique character. Oak aging, for example, can impart flavors of vanilla, spice, and toast, depending on the type of oak and its level of toasting, while stainless steel fermentation helps preserve the wine's natural fruitiness and acidity. Understanding these processes allows you to decipher the nuances within a wine and to appreciate the winemaker's skill and intention. A good wine list will often provide insights into the winemaking techniques employed, further enhancing the overall experience.

Wine tasting, while seemingly straightforward, is a refined art that requires attention to detail. The process begins with visual observation, assessing the wine's clarity, color, and how it moves in the glass. Swirling the wine allows its aromas to fully develop, setting the stage for the next step. Take a deep breath, noting the intensity and complexity of the scents. Common descriptors include fruity notes such as cherry, blackberry, or citrus; floral aromas like rose or violet; and earthy undertones such as mushroom or truffle. Finally, "take a sip and allow the wine to coat your palate. Pay attention to the wine's texture, acidity,[15]" tannin structure, balance, and length of finish, as these elements contribute to its overall complexity and quality. Note the interplay of flavors, the evolution on the palate, and the lingering aftertaste. Practice makes perfect, and with experience, you'll develop a more nuanced vocabulary to describe your sensory impressions.

Furthermore, the context in which you enjoy wine plays a significant role in the overall experience. The right glassware can enhance the aromas and flavors, while the ambiance can set the mood. A dimly lit restaurant with soft music can create a sophisticated atmosphere, allowing you to savor each sip. Conversely, a casual setting with friends can be just as enjoyable, fostering a relaxed and convivial mood. Remember, wine appreciation is a personal journey; there are no hard and fast rules. Experiment, explore, and develop your own preferences and insights.

The etiquette surrounding wine consumption adds another layer of sophistication. Knowing how to properly hold a wine glass, swirl the wine, and take a sip demonstrates refinement and respect. At a formal dinner, understanding the order in which wines are served, typically starting with lighter-bodied whites and progressing to full-bodied reds, shows awareness of established customs. Offering your companion a taste or ensuring others feel included in informal settings reflects gracious hospitality. Knowing when to refill a glass without being intrusive is a mark of thoughtful service.

Engage in informed conversation about the wine. Share your observations and, when appropriate, ask thoughtful questions of the sommelier or fellow diners. Avoid overly critical pronouncements, and instead use descriptive comments that reflect your personal experience. Respecting others' preferences is essential, as the subjective nature of wine appreciation invites a range of opinions.

Beyond social graces, understanding how to store and serve wine correctly is also important. Storing wine at the appropriate temperature helps preserve its quality and character. Red wines are best served slightly cooler than modern room temperature, while white wines are typically enjoyed lightly chilled. Knowing how to open a bottle smoothly and using a decanter when appropriate helps avoid awkward moments and enhances the overall experience. Choosing the right glassware for different types of wine also reflects a genuine appreciation and understanding of the beverage.

The world of wine extends far beyond the basics outlined here. Further exploration into specific regions, wine styles, and vintages will continually deepen your understanding and appreciation. Consider attending wine tastings, joining wine clubs, or taking a wine appreciation course to enhance your knowledge and refine your palate.

Engage with sommeliers and wine professionals, seeking their insights and guidance. Read books and articles, exploring the history, culture, and science behind winemaking. The more you learn, the more you'll appreciate the artistry and craftsmanship involved in creating a fine wine. Remember, wine appreciation is a journey of continuous discovery, a path that rewards those who approach it with curiosity, patience, and a refined sense of appreciation. The ultimate goal is not to become a wine expert overnight, but to cultivate a discerning palate and to enjoy the "rich tapestry of flavors, aromas, and experiences that the world of wine has to offer.[16]" This, in turn, allows for more engaging and informed conversations, enhancing your social interactions and demonstrating your refined sensibilities.

Finally, responsible consumption is paramount. Enjoying wine should be a pleasurable experience, not a means to excess. Knowing your limits and respecting the effects of alcohol is crucial, both for personal well-being and for maintaining the social graces associated with sophisticated enjoyment. Never drink and drive, and always be mindful of the impact alcohol can have on your judgment and behavior.

A discerning gentleman knows when to savor a glass and when to step away, ensuring the enjoyment of both the wine and the company remains central to the experience.

Wine appreciation, for the modern gentleman, is more than just drinking.

It's an exploration of history, geography, and artistry that culminates in a rich sensory experience. This journey begins with mastering the basics, laying the foundation for a sophisticated palate and insightful discussions about the art of wine appreciation.

Classic Drinks and Modern Mixology

Building upon our exploration of wine appreciation, we now delve into the equally captivating world of spirits and cocktails. While wine showcases the breadth of terroir and varietal expression, spirits offer a distillation of essence, which is a more concentrated and potent experience. Understanding spirits, like wine, goes beyond recognizing popular brands. It involves appreciating the craftsmanship, the history, and the mixologist's artistry that elevate these beverages to a form of cultural expression.

The classic spirits, including whiskey, gin, rum, vodka, tequila, and brandy, each possess distinct character shaped by their base ingredients, distillation methods, and, where applicable, aging processes. Whiskey, for instance, offers an impressive array of variations influenced by its grain source (rye, barley, corn, or wheat), maturation methods (such as American oak or sherry casks), and geographical origin, including Scotland, Ireland, the United States, and Japan. These factors create a spectrum of flavor profiles, from smoky and peaty to smooth and sweet, making whiskey a versatile and complex spirit.

Gin's defining characteristic lies in its botanical composition. Juniper berries are the primary ingredient, but the inclusion of other botanicals, such as citrus peels, coriander, cardamom, or lavender, yields diverse flavor profiles. This versatility makes gin a cornerstone of mixology, capable of lending itself to both classic and inventive cocktails. Rum, too, boasts remarkable diversity, with light, dark, and spiced varieties crafted from sugarcane and shaped by fermentation methods and oak barrel aging.

CHAPTER 6

Vodka, often perceived as neutral, serves as a blank canvas for mixologists, allowing the flavors of other ingredients to shine in innovative cocktails. Tequila, derived from the agave plant, ranges from the bright and crisp notes of a Blanco to the rich and complex character of an Añejo, offering unique textures and tastes. Brandy, distilled from wine, reflects its vinous origins, presenting flavors that range from fruity and light to bold and oaky, depending on its source and production process.

Beyond these classics, the modern mixology scene showcases a level of creativity and sophistication deserving of attention. Crafting a cocktail is not merely about combining ingredients; it requires precision, balance, and a deep understanding of flavor dynamics. Modern cocktails often incorporate fresh fruit juices, artisanal syrups, bitters, and other innovative elements, resulting in layered and nuanced flavor profiles.

A well-made cocktail strikes a harmonious balance between sweet, sour, bitter, and strong components, reflecting the bartender's skill and attention to detail. Too much emphasis on one element can overwhelm the others, disrupting the drink's equilibrium. Learning to recognize and appreciate this balance enhances your enjoyment. Understanding the history behind a classic cocktail adds another dimension to the experience, offering a glimpse into the evolution of drinking culture and the stories of innovation that have shaped it.

Take the Old Fashioned, for example, a seemingly simple drink with a rich history dating back to the 19th century. Its evolution mirrors changes in taste and style, showing how timeless classics can be reinterpreted. Similarly, the martini, a symbol of elegance and sophistication, has inspired countless variations, each tailored to its creator's vision. The method of preparation, whether stirring or shaking, the choice of glassware, and the garnish all contribute to the sensory experience, elevating the act of enjoying a cocktail into an art form.

As with wine, responsible consumption is fundamental. Enjoying spirits and cocktails should enhance, not compromise, personal safety or social interactions. Only drink in moderation, never drink and drive, and be mindful of alcohol's effects on judgment and behavior. Recognizing and respecting your limits demonstrates maturity and self-awareness, key attributes of a refined gentleman.

The setting in which you enjoy spirits also matters. A smoky whiskey by a crackling fire on a chilly evening creates a very different ambiance from a refreshing gin and tonic sipped on a warm afternoon. The occasion, the company, and the atmosphere all play a role in shaping the experience. Selecting a spirit that complements the context demonstrates thoughtfulness and a sophisticated understanding of social graces. Similarly, pairing spirits with food, much like wine pairing, introduces a new layer of enjoyment. Certain spirits can enhance the flavors of particular dishes, adding depth to the dining experience.

Exploring spirits and cocktails requires curiosity and a willingness to experiment. Venturing beyond the familiar allows you to discover new tastes and broaden your preferences. This doesn't mean amassing an extensive collection of rare bottles. Starting with the classics and experimenting with variations is an excellent way to build your knowledge. Attending cocktail-making classes offers both practical skills and theoretical insights into this intricate art form. Engaging with experienced mixologists, reading books on the subject, and visiting bars renowned for their craft cocktails are valuable ways to deepen your appreciation.

The world of spirits and cocktails is ever-evolving, with new trends and techniques continually emerging. At its core, however, lies an appreciation for craftsmanship, balance, and the artistry involved in their creation. By understanding these principles, a gentleman moves beyond simply ordering a drink to appreciating its history, craftsmanship, and the mixologist's subtle touch. This thoughtful engagement transforms spirits and cocktails into an opportunity for meaningful social interaction and is a testament to cultivated taste.

Ultimately, enjoying spirits is about more than the drink itself. It's about the experience, the conversation, and the cultivated appreciation for the finer things in life. It's a craft, an art, and a celebration of a life well-lived. Approached with curiosity, respect, and sophistication, the world of spirits and cocktails becomes yet another avenue through which a gentleman can express his refined sensibilities and enrich his social repertoire.

A Gentleman's Pursuit

The transition from the vibrant world of spirits to the quiet contemplation of a fine cigar is a natural progression for the discerning gentleman. Both represent a refined appreciation for craftsmanship, history, and the subtle nuances of sensory experience. Yet, while spirits often thrive in lively social settings, the enjoyment of a cigar invites introspection, thoughtful conversation, and a moment to savor life's quiet luxuries. Choosing the right cigar, much like selecting a fine wine, is central to the experience. It requires understanding origins, blends, and the intended sensory journey.

The world of cigars is as vast as it's intricate, offering a dazzling array of options. Understanding the basic classifications, such as size, shape (vitola), wrapper leaf, and filler, is a vital starting point. The size, measured by ring gauge (the diameter in sixty-fourths of an inch), influences the smoking experience. While larger ring gauges often provide a cooler, slower burn with more filler influence, smaller ring gauges can intensify flavors due to the higher wrapper-to-filler ratio. The vitola, or shape, affects the draw and burn rate, shaping the overall enjoyment. For instance, a Robusto's short, thick form delivers bold flavors quickly, while a Churchill's long, slender design offers a slower, more contemplative smoke.

The wrapper leaf, the cigar's outer layer, significantly influences a cigar's aroma, flavor, burn characteristics, and visual appeal, though the filler tobaccos play the primary role in shaping the overall taste profile. Wrapper types, from the rich, dark maduro to the light, delicate claro, impart distinct characteristics. Much like wine, the terroir of a cigar's tobacco—whether in the wrapper, binder, or filler—greatly influences its flavor. Regions such as Cuba, Nicaragua (notably Estelí and Jalapa), the Dominican Republic, and Honduras each impart distinct characteristics to the tobacco, from spicy and full-bodied to smooth and creamy. The filler tobaccos, forming the cigar's core, provide depth and complexity, while the binder leaf, sandwiched between filler and wrapper, ensures structural integrity and influences the draw.

Choosing the right cigar goes beyond its technical details; it's about personal preference and occasion. A full-bodied cigar with earthy notes and spice might suit a quiet evening of contemplation, while a milder blend with floral or fruity undertones complements a post-dinner conversation. A knowledgeable tobacconist is an invaluable guide, helping navigate the vast selection and recommending options tailored to your taste and the moment. Don't hesitate to seek their advice; they can greatly enhance your appreciation.

The ritual of cutting and lighting a cigar is as much a part of the experience as smoking it. Choosing the right cut affects the draw and smoking experience. A sharp guillotine cutter provides a clean, even cut, but a V-cut can concentrate the smoke for a more intense draw, while a punch cut limits airflow for a cooler burn. Avoid using teeth or dull cutters, as these can damage the cigar and compromise the smoking experience. Lighting, too, is a deliberate act. Use a butane torch or cedar spill, avoiding lighter fluids that might taint the flavor. Toast the foot of the cigar evenly before drawing gently to ensure a consistent burn. Remember, cigar smoke is meant to be savored in the mouth, not inhaled into the lungs.

The art of cigar enjoyment lies in savoring its subtleties. Before lighting, take in the aroma of the unlit tobacco; it provides clues to the flavors awaiting you. Once lit, take slow, deliberate puffs, letting the smoke linger to appreciate its complexity. Note the interplay of flavors as they evolve, from spices and wood to earthiness and sweetness. A well-crafted cigar offers a harmonious balance, with its flavors unfolding like a story over time. The draw, burn rate, and texture all contribute to the sensory experience, rewarding attention and patience.

Setting is also key to cigar enjoyment. A quiet, comfortable space paired with a glass of fine whiskey or brandy provides the perfect ambiance for reflection. Good company and engaging conversation can elevate the experience, but always be considerate of others. Many locations prohibit smoking and, even where allowed, it's important to respect the comfort of those nearby. Allowing the ash to build slightly before tapping it off gently helps maintain an even burn. Always dispose of ashes and remnants responsibly, demonstrating both etiquette and respect for shared spaces.

Cigar appreciation extends beyond the immediate sensory experience to the history, culture, and craftsmanship behind it. Learning about the origins of the tobacco, the traditions of cigar making, and the skill of the artisans adds depth to your enjoyment. Every cigar carries a story, more exactly a testament to heritage and artistry. Appreciating this connection transcends smoking, creating a link to a rich cultural tradition.

Cigars also provide a respite from the fast pace of modern life. The unhurried ritual of preparation, the deliberate pace of smoking, and the opportunity for quiet reflection offer a welcome escape from constant connectivity. It's a moment to disconnect from distractions, reconnect with oneself, and savor life's simple pleasures. This pause allows for introspection, a chance to reflect on experiences and appreciate the finer aspects of existence.

To truly appreciate cigars, a gentleman must develop a discerning palate and a thoughtful approach. This journey involves exploring a variety of blends, noting their nuances, and discovering personal preferences. Keeping a journal of your experiences, such as recording flavors, strengths, and impressions, can deepen your understanding and enhance your ability to choose cigars that suit your evolving taste. This practice not only enriches your enjoyment but also fosters engaging conversations with fellow enthusiasts.

Cigar enjoyment, when approached thoughtfully, is more than just smoking. It's an affirmation of a cultivated life. It reflects an appreciation for fine craftsmanship, offers moments of quiet reflection, and invites the sharing of a sensory experience in good company. It's an art that complements a gentleman's refined tastes, adding depth and sophistication to his lifestyle. A well-chosen cigar speaks volumes about one's character and attention to detail, marking him as a man of discerning taste and cultivated manners.

Ultimately, cigar appreciation is about embracing the nuances of life's finer pleasures. Through this considered approach, a gentleman finds not only enjoyment in the act but also a deeper connection to the traditions and artistry behind it. It's a hallmark of the modern gentleman, more specifically a testament to his thoughtful engagement with the world and his dedication to a life well-lived.

Moderation and Awareness

The sophisticated gentleman understands that the enjoyment of fine wines, spirits, and cigars is deeply intertwined with responsible consumption. It's not merely about indulging in luxury but it's about appreciating craftsmanship, respecting tradition, and acknowledging the potential impact of these pleasures on oneself and others. Moderation, self-awareness, and an acute understanding of context are the cornerstones of this balanced approach.

The allure of these refined pleasures lies in their capacity to enhance social interactions, inspire meaningful conversations, and provide moments of quiet reflection. Yet, overindulgence can quickly erode these benefits, leading to impaired judgment, inappropriate behavior, and health consequences. The true connoisseur embraces this delicate balance, fostering a relationship with these indulgences that is both enjoyable and responsible.

Responsible consumption begins with mindful pacing. A slow, deliberate approach allows for a richer appreciation of the nuances in each drink or cigar. It enables the palate to fully explore the intricate aromas, flavors, and textures, transforming consumption into a sensory journey rather than a hurried act. This intentionality extends beyond the immediate experience, fostering introspection and a deeper understanding of one's limits and tolerances. Recognizing when to stop is as vital as knowing when to begin.

The setting significantly influences responsible consumption. A formal dinner demands a different approach than a casual evening among friends. Understanding the social context ensures that these pleasures enhance the ambiance rather than detract from it. For instance, a robust red wine pairs beautifully with a hearty meal, while a lighter aperitif suits a pre-dinner gathering. When savoring a cigar, one should be mindful of the environment and the comfort of those nearby. Consideration for others reflects not only good etiquette but also the essence of responsible behavior.

Self-awareness is at the heart of responsible enjoyment. Understanding personal limits, both physical and emotional, is crucial. This includes recognizing individual tolerances for alcohol, being mindful of the effects of different spirits and wines, and understanding the impact of nicotine. Beyond the physical, it also involves acknowledging emotional triggers and vulnerabilities. Maintaining control over mood, judgment, and decision-making may safeguard against overindulgence and its potential consequences. The responsible gentleman respects these boundaries, ensuring that indulgence remains a positive experience.

Responsibility extends beyond personal consumption to include the broader social and environmental impact of these products. Supporting producers who prioritize sustainable practices and ethical sourcing is a vital aspect of mindful enjoyment. Choosing wines from vineyards employing eco-friendly techniques, spirits from distilleries committed to fair labor practices, and cigars crafted with sustainably sourced tobacco demonstrates a conscientious approach. This consideration reflects a deeper understanding of how individual choices impact the environment and society at large.

Informed choices enrich the experience of fine indulgences. Understanding the origins of a wine, the distillation process of a spirit, or the cultivation of cigar tobacco deepens appreciation for the artistry involved. Knowing the nuances of grape varietals, whiskey aging, or cigar tobaccos transforms consumption into a journey of discovery. This knowledge enables thoughtful selection and fosters engaging conversations, elevating the act of indulgence to an art form.

The responsible gentleman prioritizes the safety and well-being of himself and others. This includes never driving under the influence, refraining from pressuring others to consume, and always ensuring the safety of companions. Awareness of potential health risks and a commitment to mitigating them further underscore the importance of moderation. Responsible enjoyment is fundamentally about mindfulness and respect, for oneself, for others, and for the context.

Beyond sensory pleasure, the refined appreciation of wines, spirits, and cigars connects the individual to a rich tapestry of history, culture, and craftsmanship. Understanding the heritage of a wine region, the traditions of spirit-making, or the meticulous art of cigar production adds layers of meaning to the experience. This connection elevates indulgence into an exploration of human ingenuity and tradition, fostering a profound respect for the artistry behind these pleasures.

Responsible consumption is not necessarily about abstinence; it's about cultivating a mindful relationship with life's finer pleasures. It's an expression of balance, intentionality, and sophistication. Savoring each moment, respecting personal limits, and appreciating how the craft transforms indulgence into a celebration of life's simple luxuries. Moderation and self-awareness are not constraints but essential elements of true enjoyment, enriching both the individual and their social interactions.

The discerning gentleman approaches these refined pleasures with a thoughtful understanding of their impact. This measured approach reflects a broader philosophy of balanced living; one that values quality over quantity and engagement over excess. The choice to indulge is an opportunity to savor, appreciate, and connect. In doing so, the gentleman elevates the enjoyment of wines, spirits, and cigars to moments of refined contemplation and responsible pleasure. This mindful approach is the hallmark of a cultivated life; a testament to the art of living well.

Enhancing Culinary Experiences

The appreciation of fine wines, spirits, and cigars extends far beyond savoring their individual characteristics. A true connoisseur understands the transformative power of pairing these indulgences with complementary foods, creating a multi-sensory experience that elevates the pleasure to new heights. This art of pairing is not about adhering to rigid rules but rather embracing a nuanced understanding of how flavors, aromas, and textures interact harmoniously.

Consider the timeless pairing of a robust Cabernet Sauvignon with a grilled steak. The tannins in the wine, which create a drying sensation on the palate, bind with the proteins in the steak, softening the perception of astringency while the fat in the meat smooths out the wine's structure. This interplay enhances both the wine and the dish, creating a balanced and satisfying experience. The wine's blackcurrant, cedar, and vanilla notes echo and enhance the steak's savory profile, while its full-bodied nature provides a satisfying counterpoint to the meat's texture. Conversely, a delicate Pinot Noir may struggle against the steak's bold flavors, while a more robust Zinfandel could overshadow its nuances. However, richer styles of Pinot Noir from warmer regions, such as California or New Zealand, can pair beautifully with leaner cuts like filet mignon. Achieving a successful pairing depends on carefully considering weight, acidity, tannins, and the flavor profiles of both the food and beverage.

This principle applies just as aptly to lighter fare. The interplay between a crisp Sauvignon Blanc and fresh oysters demonstrates this beautifully. The wine's bright acidity balances the oysters' briny richness, while its grassy, citrusy notes complement the subtle flavors of the sea. Minerality in the wine further enhances the impression, resulting in a refreshing and elegant combination. Similarly, the buttery texture and tropical notes of a Chardonnay make it a natural companion for rich seafood like lobster or scallops, creating a luxurious, cohesive experience.

Spirits also lend themselves to thoughtful pairing. A smoky Islay scotch, known for its peat-forward character, pairs perfectly with hearty dishes like venison stew. The intensity of the scotch aligns with the richness of the meat, while its smoky undertones mirror the earthy depth of the dish. Conversely, a light, floral gin with botanicals such as cucumber or elderflower pairs best in cocktails with seafood or a summer salad. When mixed with tonic or citrus-based mixers, its refreshing qualities enhance the meal's delicacy without overpowering it. The key lies in balancing the intensity of the spirit with the complexity of the dish.

Texture plays a crucial role in pairing as well. A creamy cheese, such as Brie or Camembert, pairs beautifully with wines that provide contrast rather than mirroring its richness. A crisp, acidic Chardonnay or a dry sparkling wine like Champagne cuts through the creaminess, creating a balanced experience. Meanwhile, a late-harvest Riesling or Sauternes pairs better with salty or pungent cheeses, such as blue cheese, where the wine's sweetness offsets the bold flavors. The textures meld seamlessly, creating a harmonious and memorable mouthfeel. On the other hand, crumbly cheeses often benefit from wines with higher acidity or tannins, which cut through their richness and refresh the palate.

Cigars introduce another layer of complexity to pairing. A robust, full-bodied cigar, rich with bold tobacco flavors, calls for a drink that can hold its own. A sweet, dark port wine, with its notes of dried fruit and chocolate, complements the cigar's spice and strength. Meanwhile, a lighter cigar might pair better with a gentler spirit like cognac or rum, whose subtle sweetness enhances the cigar's more delicate qualities without overpowering them.

Context is equally important when considering pairings. A casual gathering might call for a relaxed approach, such as pairing a crisp beer with appetizers, while a formal dinner party invites meticulous attention to detail with carefully curated wines accompanying each course. The setting, company, and ambiance all inform the choices, ensuring the pairing enhances the overall experience.

Beyond the technicalities of flavor and texture, the art of pairing is about curating an experience, namely as a sequence of sensory impressions that create a cohesive and memorable moment. This orchestration of flavors elevates the act of dining into a culinary symphony. For instance, a meal might progress from a light aperitif to a crisp white wine with seafood, a full-bodied red with the main course and, finally, a dessert wine and a cigar. Each element builds upon the previous, culminating in a crescendo of sensory delight.

Temperature plays a pivotal role in maximizing enjoyment. A chilled white wine served too warm loses its vibrancy, while an overly cold red wine fails to release its aromatic bouquet. Similarly, serving spirits at their optimal temperature enhances their flavors and aromas, ensuring a balanced and enjoyable experience. Attention to such details can make or break a pairing.

Experimentation is vital in mastering this art. Trying new combinations, exploring varied flavor profiles, and noting how components interact can reveal surprising and delightful pairings. Starting with established combinations and branching out gradually allows the development of a refined palate and personal preferences. Keeping a journal to document observations and preferences aids in honing this skill, making the journey as rewarding as the destination.

The art of pairing is more than a technical skill; it's a creative endeavor requiring an intuitive grasp of flavor, texture, and aroma, as well as an appreciation of context. It's about crafting a holistic sensory experience that engages the senses and leaves a lasting impression. Successful pairing showcases a refined palate and a sophisticated understanding of culinary arts, hallmarks of a discerning gentleman. Over time, this skill enhances social interactions, impresses guests, and deepens personal enjoyment of life's finer pleasures. It transcends taste, creating lasting memories and moments of shared enjoyment.

Ultimately, pairing fine wines, spirits, and cigars with complementary foods celebrates the intersection of gastronomy and conviviality. It demonstrates the gentleman's dedication to cultivating refined pleasures with thoughtful intention, creating not just meals, but meaningful experiences. This nuanced art embodies sophistication and elevates indulgence into a celebration of life's richness.

Chapter 7

Travel Etiquette – Navigating Global Settings

Customs and Cultural Nuances

International travel offers unparalleled opportunities for personal and professional growth, broadening perspectives and fostering intercultural understanding. However, navigating diverse cultural landscapes requires sensitivity, awareness, and a willingness to adapt. Success in international travel hinges on understanding and respecting the customs and nuances of the countries you visit. This isn't just about avoiding faux pas; it's about demonstrating respect, building rapport, and fostering positive interactions.

A crucial aspect of international travel etiquette involves nonverbal communication. Gestures, posture, and eye contact carry vastly different meanings across cultures. A friendly gesture in one country might be offensive elsewhere. For instance, the "thumbs up" sign, widely positive in Western countries, is considered vulgar in parts of the Middle East and South America. Similarly, while direct eye contact is valued in Western cultures as a sign of confidence, it can be perceived as aggressive in certain Asian cultures. Before traveling, research common nonverbal cues and adjust your behavior accordingly. Cultural guides, online resources, and conversations with experienced travelers can provide valuable insight.

Beyond nonverbal communication, understanding local customs is essential. This includes greetings, introductions, dining etiquette, and gift-giving traditions. In many Asian cultures, bowing is customary, with the depth and duration signifying respect. In some Middle Eastern countries, greetings involve a handshake, often accompanied by a light kiss on each cheek. Ignoring these norms can be seen as disrespectful. Dining etiquette also varies widely. In some cultures, leaving a small amount of food on your plate signifies satisfaction, while in others, finishing everything is a sign of appreciation. Researching these nuances beforehand helps navigate social situations with confidence and ease.

Dressing appropriately is another key consideration. While comfort is important, local dress codes must be respected, particularly at religious sites and formal events. In certain countries, modest attire is expected, requiring covered shoulders, knees, or even hair. Ignoring these expectations can cause misunderstandings or offense. Packing versatile clothing that adapts to different situations is a practical approach. Travel blogs, guidebooks, and insights from locals can help ensure appropriate attire for any occasion.

Respect for local religions and beliefs is equally important. Many countries have strong religious traditions and demonstrating sensitivity is crucial. This might mean dressing modestly at religious sites, refraining from public displays of affection, and observing customs during religious holidays. Conversations about religion should be approached carefully and only if initiated by locals. Being aware of and respecting religious customs avoids potential offenses while fostering cultural understanding and empathy.

Navigating international business etiquette is another vital skill. Meeting structures, communication styles, and negotiation tactics differ across cultures. Some business environments adhere to strict formalities and agendas, while others take a more relaxed approach. Researching cultural norms before business engagements is essential, including appropriate levels of formality, preferred communication channels, and acceptable negotiation strategies. Understanding these nuances enhances professional interactions and contributes to successful business dealings abroad.

Awareness of local laws and regulations is crucial. This includes visa requirements, customs regulations, and laws concerning behavior and attire. Failing to comply can lead to fines, imprisonment, or deportation. Preparing well in advance ensures a smooth travel experience. Understanding customs regulations prevents issues with restricted items, while knowledge of local laws regarding conduct, dress, and public behavior helps avoid unintentional offenses.

Learning a few basic phrases in the local language is a meaningful gesture. Fluency isn't necessary, but simple phrases like "hello", "thank you", and "excuse me" demonstrate respect and a willingness to engage. Making an effort to speak the local language fosters positive interactions and enriches the travel experience. Language learning apps or short courses can be valuable investments before a trip.

Finally, adopting a mindset of humility and openness is key. Recognizing that your cultural perspective is just one of many allows for meaningful interactions and deeper understanding. Approach each experience with curiosity and respect, embracing cultural differences with an open mind. This attitude enhances travel experiences, fosters genuine connections, and leaves a lasting positive impression on both visitors and locals. Engaging with individuals on a personal level provides a broader, more authentic understanding of a culture, making international travel not only enjoyable but truly enriching.

Efficiency and Respect

Airports, bustling hubs of global connectivity, can feel like pressure cookers of stress and impatience. Yet, navigating these environments with grace and efficiency is entirely achievable. It's about understanding unspoken rules, anticipating potential delays, and demonstrating a level of consideration that reflects well on you personally and professionally. A modern gentleman understands that even in chaotic settings, composure and respect are paramount.

Preparation is key. Before stepping into the airport, check in online, download your boarding pass, and confirm your gate location. These preemptive steps minimize anxiety and prevent frantic last-minute rushes that lead to frayed tempers and poor behavior. Knowing your flight details allows for a calmer, more collected approach, setting the tone for a pleasant journey. Anticipate potential delays by packing essentials such as a book, noise-canceling headphones, and a portable charger to turn downtime into a productive or relaxing experience.

Upon arrival, maintain a mindful pace. Rushing through crowds increases the risk of collisions and projects a frantic energy that unsettles others. Move with purpose but also consideration, staying aware of your surroundings and the space you occupy. A composed demeanor is always more effective than hurried aggression.

Security checkpoints often breed frustration, but preparation eases the process. Keep liquids and electronics readily accessible, remove shoes and belts proactively, and follow instructions attentively. More importantly, be patient. Security personnel are doing a crucial job, and courtesy goes a long way. A simple "thank you" can turn a tense interaction into a pleasant one. Avoid grumbling or sarcastic remarks, which only add unnecessary negativity. Treat security staff with the same level of respect you expect in any professional setting.

CHAPTER 7

Navigating baggage check-in requires forethought. Ensure your luggage is clearly labeled with your name and contact information. Use durable, easily identifiable tags. If traveling with oversized or unusually shaped baggage, be prepared for additional processing time. Should an issue arise, remain polite and patient because effective communication resolves problems quickly. Treating airline staff with respect is polite and helps ensure a smooth check-in process.

Once past security, locating your gate efficiently requires some navigational awareness. Familiarize yourself with the airport's layout through an app or printed directory. While asking for directions is fine, when necessary, self-reliance projects confidence and minimizes the burden on staff handling multiple concerns. Respecting their time contributes to a smoother overall experience.

At the gate, be mindful of personal space. Avoid spreading your belongings unnecessarily and stay conscious of your proximity to others, especially in crowded areas. Thoughtful use of space demonstrates respect for fellow passengers, reducing friction and making the wait more pleasant for everyone.

Boarding the plane with courtesy is equally important. Allow elderly passengers, those with disabilities, and families with young children to board first when possible. Avoid rushing, and be mindful of those moving around you. When reaching your seat, be considerate of others needing access to their row. Stow your luggage promptly, ensuring it does not block the aisle. During the flight, minimize disturbances by keeping conversations at a moderate volume and setting devices to silent. Thoughtfulness toward fellow travelers fosters a more serene journey for all.

Exiting the airport is another opportunity to demonstrate impeccable manners. At the baggage claim, retrieve your luggage promptly and move away from the carousel to allow others easy access. Avoid lingering unnecessarily.

Be courteous to baggage handlers and airport staff, acknowledging their assistance with a simple "thank you".

Airports, though hectic, are a microcosm of society, and your actions reflect your character and social awareness. By prioritizing preparation, consideration, and respect, you can navigate these environments with grace, leaving a positive impression on those around you and enhancing your own travel experience. Even in stressful circumstances, the mark of a true gentleman is his ability to maintain composure, empathy, and courtesy. This is not merely about following rules but about demonstrating respect for others and elevating travel from a necessity to a refined experience.

Professionalism and Courtesy

The transition from the structured environment of an airport to the relative calm, or potential chaos, of a hotel requires a subtle shift in etiquette. While the principles of respect and consideration remain constant, their application adapts to the new setting. A hotel, a temporary home away from home, demands professionalism and courtesy, not only toward the staff but also toward fellow guests.

Upon arrival, approach the reception desk with confidence and composure. Avoid appearing rushed or flustered, even if time is tight. A simple, polite "Good afternoon" or "Good evening", followed by a clear statement of your reservation details, sets the right tone. If you have special requests, such as a higher floor, a specific view, or accessibility accommodations, you should express them clearly and courteously, keeping in mind that they are requests, not entitlements. Regardless of the outcome, a genuine "Thank you" for their assistance is a hallmark of good manners.

Once in your room, take a moment to familiarize yourself with the hotel's amenities and services. Reviewing the provided information, including house rules, emergency contacts, and the room service menu, demonstrates

CHAPTER 7

awareness and helps facilitate a seamless stay.

Interactions with hotel staff should always reflect a sense of professional courtesy. Addressing them with respect, using appropriate titles such as "Mr.", "Ms.", "Sir", or "Madam", unless they suggest otherwise, fosters a positive dynamic. If a staff member introduces themselves by name, remembering it adds a personal touch that is always appreciated. A warm smile and a simple "please" and "thank you" go a long way in creating a pleasant exchange.

When requesting services, clarity and conciseness are key. Rather than saying, "My room is cold," a more effective approach would be, "Could you please adjust the thermostat in room 312? It seems to be set too low." Providing precise information helps avoid misunderstandings and ensures efficient assistance.

Tipping is another important aspect of hotel etiquette. Customary amounts vary by country, so it's advisable to research local expectations in advance. While there's no obligation to over-tip, a reasonable gratuity for room service, housekeeping, or bellhop assistance is a thoughtful way to acknowledge their efforts.

Consideration should also extend to fellow guests. Keeping noise levels to a minimum, particularly late at night, demonstrates an awareness of shared space. Respecting hotel quiet hours, avoiding disruptive behavior, and maintaining a general sense of decorum contribute to a more pleasant experience for everyone.

When using hotel amenities, treating the space with care is essential. Furniture, fixtures, and equipment should be used responsibly, and any malfunctions or damage should be reported promptly to prevent inconvenience for future guests. Shared facilities such as the gym or pool require additional attentiveness, such as cleaning up after oneself and following posted guidelines ensures that these areas remain enjoyable for all.

For those traveling on business, professionalism extends beyond meeting rooms. Conducting oneself with discretion in public areas, keeping phone calls at an appropriate volume, and dressing suitably, even in casual settings, all contribute to the impression one leaves behind. A hotel lobby or lounge is often an informal meeting ground, making composure and self-awareness essential.

If an issue arises with your room or service, addressing it with patience and politeness is far more effective than adopting a confrontational tone. Explaining concerns calmly and clearly increases the likelihood of a swift resolution. If a matter remains unresolved, following the hotel's complaint procedures is more productive than a public display of dissatisfaction.

Technology use within the hotel environment also requires mindfulness. Speakerphone conversations in public areas can be disruptive, and excessive downloading or streaming can impact Wi-Fi access for other guests. Keeping mobile device usage discreet and non-intrusive ensures that shared spaces remain comfortable for all.

Departure should be as polished as arrival. Settling the bill promptly, double-checking charges, and leaving the room in a tidy state reflect well on you as a guest. Expressing gratitude to the staff with a final "Thank you" and a courteous farewell is a simple yet impactful gesture.

Hotel etiquette is not just about following rules. It's about demonstrating consideration, professionalism, and respect for both the space and the people within it. By embracing these principles, you enhance your own travel experience and contribute to a more pleasant atmosphere for those around you. A modern gentleman understands that even in a transient setting, impeccable manners elevate his personal brand and leave a lasting impression.

CHAPTER 7

Adapting to Cultural Differences

The transition from the polished comfort of a hotel to the vibrant, often unpredictable landscape of a foreign dining experience requires both adaptability and cultural awareness. While the principles of courtesy and respect remain universal, their application varies dramatically depending on the cultural context. Overlooking these nuances can lead to awkward misunderstandings or, worse, unintended offense. The modern gentleman must therefore approach international dining with an open mind and a willingness to learn.

This is not merely about avoiding faux pas; it's about demonstrating respect for the host culture, showcasing adaptability, and deepening one's understanding of global traditions. In many societies, the dining table is more than a place for sustenance. It's a social hub, a setting for forging relationships, and a reflection of national values. Engaging with these customs allows one to participate in a meaningful cross-cultural dialogue, enriching the travel experience immeasurably.

One of the first considerations is punctuality. Some cultures operate on a flexible notion of time, while others adhere to strict schedules. Arriving excessively early may disrupt your host's preparations, whereas tardiness could be seen as disrespectful. A well-informed gentleman strives for punctuality, understanding that even a minor delay may be interpreted differently depending on the culture.

Seating arrangements also vary. In some traditions, the head of the table holds a position of honor, in others, seniority or guest status dictates placement. Observing and following the host's lead is essential. Insisting on a particular seat or hesitating excessively can be perceived as a lack of deference. Allowing yourself to be guided demonstrates humility and an understanding of social hierarchy.

The use of utensils and dining practices further illustrates cultural diversity. Chopsticks require delicate precision in many Asian cultures, while in some regions, eating with one's hands is customary. Western table settings follow a structured sequence of fork and knife use, which may not align with other traditions. While it's impossible to master every nuance beforehand, making an effort to learn basic etiquette will be appreciated. When in doubt, observing and mirroring your host's actions is a subtle yet effective way to show respect.

Even the act of eating carries symbolic meaning. In certain cultures, leaving a small amount of food on one's plate signifies satisfaction, while in others, a clean plate demonstrates appreciation for the meal. Understanding these distinctions helps prevent unintended misinterpretations. Adaptability and keen observation are key.

Conversation at the table is equally nuanced. Some cultures encourage animated discussions, while others favor a more reserved atmosphere. Gauging the mood of your hosts and adjusting accordingly prevents social missteps. Loud or overly boisterous behavior may be frowned upon in some settings, while in others, a lively exchange is expected. Similarly, certain topics, such as politics or religion, may be off-limits, requiring discretion and cultural sensitivity.

The offering and acceptance of food and drink warrant particular attention. In many cultures, accepting with both hands is a sign of respect, acknowledging both the giver and the food itself. Refusing an offering can sometimes be perceived as a slight. If dietary restrictions exist, communicating them politely in advance ensures clarity without offending one's host.

Tipping customs also vary widely. In some countries, gratuities are expected, while in others, they are considered unnecessary or even inappropriate. Researching local norms before dining eliminates awkward moments and ensures adherence to proper etiquette.

CHAPTER 7

Beyond the practicalities, dining abroad is an opportunity for cultural exchange. Observing, learning, and appreciating the subtleties of a meal fosters deeper connections. Asking polite questions, expressing genuine interest in the cuisine, and engaging in respectful conversation enhance the experience.

Consider, for example, a formal dinner in Japan, where meticulous preparation and presentation extend beyond the food to encompass the entire dining ritual. From the precise placement of chopsticks to the ceremonial pouring of sake, each action carries cultural significance. A gentleman's attentiveness to these details signals respect and appreciation. Conversely, a casual meal in Italy might involve animated conversation and expressive gestures, where participation in lively discourse is not only welcomed but expected.

Similar distinctions exist in Southeast Asia, where the concept of "face" governs social interactions. Demonstrating respect for elders and authority figures, whether through conversation or the handling of food, carries weight. A simple act of deference, such as allowing others to serve themselves first, conveys cultural awareness and consideration.

In many Middle Eastern cultures, hospitality is central to the dining experience. Meals are often communal, and refusing food or drink can be perceived as impolite. Expressing sincere gratitude and engaging warmly with the host's generosity is essential. Additionally, in some cultures, using the right hand for eating and serving is a sign of respect.

Ultimately, dining etiquette abroad is not merely a set of rules but a pathway to deeper cultural understanding. By embracing these experiences with curiosity and a willingness to adapt, the modern gentleman transforms a simple meal into an opportunity for meaningful interaction. Respect, empathy, and a sincere desire to learn from others, elevate the experience beyond sustenance, turning dining into a bridge for lasting connections and mutual appreciation.

Public Transit and Private Vehicles

The transition from the refined elegance of a five-star restaurant to the often-chaotic reality of public transportation requires an adjustment in etiquette. While the principles of courtesy and respect remain unchanged, their application must adapt to the shared space and diverse population found in buses, trains, and subways. In these environments, consideration for others is paramount.

Offering your seat to the elderly, pregnant women, or those with disabilities is not merely a polite gesture but it's a demonstration of respect for those who may need assistance. Beyond physical considerations, being mindful of your noise levels is essential. Avoid loud conversations, boisterous laughter, or the intrusive blare of personal audio devices. Recognizing the communal nature of public transit, a gentleman minimizes disruptions to fellow travelers.

The use of personal electronic devices also requires discretion. While checking emails or engaging in quiet activities is acceptable, prolonged phone calls impose on others' peace. The bright glare of a smartphone or tablet can be distracting, so moderating screen brightness and duration of use is a thoughtful touch. Eating and drinking on public transit demand similar consideration because strong odors or messy foods should be avoided. A gentleman carries a handkerchief for unexpected spills and disposes of any waste responsibly, ensuring public spaces remain clean and orderly.

Etiquette in Hired Cars and Private Transport

When travelling abroad, a gentleman will often rely on chauffeured cars, ride-share services, or hired vehicles. Each requires a standard of courtesy that reflects both personal character and cultural awareness.

With chauffeured or car services, punctuality is essential. A gentleman ensures he is ready at the appointed time, greets his driver politely, and states his destination clearly. Excessive instructions or unnecessary demands diminish professionalism. If the culture calls for it, tipping should be discreet and respectful.

With ride-share services, courtesy begins the moment you enter the vehicle. A warm greeting, maintaining a clean presence, and speaking at a considerate volume all signal respect. If conversation arises, keep it polite and neutral, avoiding divisive or overly personal topics.

With hired cars abroad, a gentleman confirms details of insurance and agreements before departure and returns the vehicle in good order. Observing local driving customs is as important as obeying traffic laws, for what is acceptable at home may be considered discourteous elsewhere.

In every form of private transport, the principle is the same: respect the time, space, and effort of others. Gratitude, whether expressed through words, gestures, or conduct, transforms a simple journey into an experience that reflects polish and consideration.

Cultural Sensitivities in Transportation

Navigating different cultures requires attentiveness to local norms. In some countries, offering a seat to an elder carries deep social significance. In others, public displays of affection, even in private vehicles, may be frowned upon. A well-traveled gentleman researches these customs in advance, turning potential misunderstandings into opportunities for cultural exchange and personal growth.

Understanding local transportation systems is equally important. Familiarizing oneself with ticketing procedures, fare structures, and behavioral expectations prevents missteps and demonstrates respect for local customs. Choosing the most appropriate mode of transport is also key, while hailing a taxi may be common in some cities, public transit may be the more practical and culturally appropriate option elsewhere.

The Broader Perspective

Ultimately, transportation etiquette is about more than adhering to rules; it reflects a broader philosophy of respect, awareness, and harmonious coexistence. A gentleman considers his impact on those around him, striving to create positive travel experiences for all. Whether navigating a bustling metropolis or a rural landscape, his ability to adapt with grace and consideration defines his character.

By practicing these principles, he enhances not only his own journey but also the experiences of those around him, reinforcing his role as a responsible global citizen. The modern gentleman's ability to navigate varied situations with dignity, cultural awareness, and unwavering respect remains a testament to his character and commitment to refined living.

Chapter 8

Digital Decorum – Navigating the Online World

Crafting a Professional Image

In today's interconnected world, your online presence often serves as your first impression; a digital handshake that precedes any face-to-face interaction. Whether you're connecting with a potential employer, a client, or a new acquaintance, your online image should be carefully curated to reflect your values, skills, and aspirations. Building a professional presence isn't just about being on multiple platforms; it's about crafting a cohesive and compelling narrative that reinforces your credibility.

A strong online presence starts with understanding your target audience. Who are you trying to reach? Are you seeking career opportunities, expanding your professional network, or building a personal brand? Your audience dictates which platforms you prioritize and what type of content you share. For example, a marketing professional might focus on LinkedIn and Instagram to showcase industry insights and creative content, whereas an academic may find more value in specialized forums.

Once you've identified your audience, audit your existing online presence. Review your profiles across LinkedIn, Facebook, Twitter, Instagram, and any other platforms where you're active. Approach this with a critical eye. How would a potential employer or client perceive you? Are your profile pictures professional and up to date? Is your bio clear and compelling? Does your content align with your professional goals? Are there any posts or comments that could be misinterpreted or seen as unprofessional?

Remove anything that could damage your reputation, whether it's outdated content, controversial opinions, or posts that don't reflect your current goals. A single poorly judged post can have lasting consequences. Adjust privacy settings, delete unnecessary content, or even deactivate accounts that no longer serve a purpose. Proactively managing your digital footprint is essential in maintaining a polished and professional image.

Consistency is key when cultivating your online persona. Profile pictures and bios should maintain a uniform, professional appearance across all platforms. The content you share should align with your personal and professional brand, even on less formal platforms. A lighthearted post on a personal account may seem harmless, but if it contradicts the image you're building elsewhere, it can undermine your credibility.

LinkedIn, as a professional networking platform, deserves special attention. Ensure your profile is complete with a high-quality headshot, a compelling summary of your skills and experience, and detailed descriptions of past roles and achievements. Use industry-relevant keywords, actively engage with your network, and contribute valuable insights through posts, comments, and group discussions. Think of LinkedIn as more than just an online resume but more as a platform for thought leadership and relationship-building.

Other platforms like Twitter and Instagram, while less formal, also require thoughtful curation. Share valuable insights, participate in relevant conversations, and demonstrate engagement within your field. Avoid oversharing personal content or engaging in controversial debates. Even seemingly harmless posts can be misinterpreted or taken out of context, potentially harming your professional reputation.

Beyond social media, consider the broader impact of your online presence. Google yourself. What do the search results say about you? Are they aligned with the image you want to project? Address inaccuracies or outdated information where possible. Managing your online reputation is an ongoing process that requires vigilance.

Staying informed about best practices for digital professionalism is essential in an ever-evolving online landscape. Read up on online etiquette, follow industry discussions on reputation management, and attend workshops or webinars. The goal isn't just to maintain a professional presence but also to actively cultivate a strong digital brand that enhances your credibility and career prospects.

Diversifying your online presence beyond traditional social media can also strengthen your brand. Contribute to industry blogs, participate in online forums, or create a personal website to showcase your work and expertise. Writing guest posts or engaging in professional discussions can enhance your reputation and create opportunities for networking.

Visual content is another powerful tool. High-quality images and videos can elevate your online presence, making your profiles more engaging and professional. Use polished headshots for profile pictures and ensure that any visuals you share are well-composed and relevant to your brand. Attention to detail in presentation reflects professionalism.

However, professionalism extends beyond curated content since it includes responsible online behavior. Practicing digital citizenship means respecting intellectual property rights, maintaining online etiquette, and avoiding any form of cyberbullying or harassment. Your actions online carry real-world consequences, and your behavior in digital spaces is a direct reflection of your character.

Engaging in online discussions and debates requires tact and professionalism. Express dissenting opinions respectfully, avoid inflammatory language, and steer clear of personal attacks. How you handle criticism or disagreements online can significantly impact how you're perceived. A calm and professional response to negative feedback can strengthen your reputation rather than damage it.

Another crucial aspect of maintaining a professional online presence is safeguarding your digital footprint. Use strong passwords, update your software regularly, and be mindful of the personal information you share. Adjust privacy settings appropriately and think before posting. Once something is online, it's often permanent. Taking a cautious and deliberate approach demonstrates responsibility and awareness.

Crafting a professional online image is an ongoing process that requires consistency, strategic thinking, and attention to detail. By carefully managing your presence, refining your content, and staying mindful of your digital footprint, you'll develop a strong online brand that supports your career goals and enhances your reputation. Your online presence is a significant extension of your professional identity. Invest in it wisely, and it will pay dividends in your success.

Professionalism in Digital Communication

Email, once a formal mode of communication, has become a staple in both professional and personal settings. However, the rise of instant messaging and social media hasn't diminished the importance of maintaining proper etiquette in email correspondence. In fact, the speed and convenience of email amplify the risk of misinterpretation. A poorly written or improperly formatted email can undermine your credibility and strain professional relationships before a single word is spoken in person. Mastering professional email etiquette is an essential skill for navigating today's digital world.

At the core of professional email etiquette is clarity, conciseness, and courtesy. Before composing a message, consider your audience and the purpose of your communication. Are you addressing a superior, a peer, or a subordinate? Is this a routine update, a formal request, or a sensitive discussion? Understanding the context helps determine the appropriate tone and level of formality. While a casual tone may be acceptable among colleagues, a request to a senior executive requires a more polished approach.

The subject line, often overlooked, serves as your email's digital handshake. It should be concise, informative, and reflective of the email's content. Vague phrases like "Checking In" or "Quick Question" should be avoided in favor of clear, action-oriented subjects. Instead of "Project Update", opt for "Project X – Status Report and Next Steps". A well-crafted subject line makes your email easily identifiable and ensures it won't get lost in a crowded inbox.

Once the subject line is set, the body of the email should be equally well-structured. Begin with a polite salutation that matches the formality of your relationship with the recipient. "Dear Mr./Ms./Mx. [Last Name]" is standard in professional settings unless you have an established informal rapport. Overly casual greetings like "Hey" or "Hi" may come across as unprofessional in more formal interactions.

The message itself should be direct and well-organized. Use clear, straightforward language, avoiding jargon or overly technical terms that the recipient may not understand.[17] Break up lengthy paragraphs to improve readability and, when appropriate, use bullet points or numbered lists to highlight key information. Respect the recipient's time by getting to the point and eliminating unnecessary details.

Grammar and spelling are critical. Errors can make you appear careless and unprofessional. Before sending an email, proofread it carefully. While grammar and spell-check tools are helpful, they aren't foolproof; always conduct a final manual review. Taking this extra step demonstrates attention to detail and respect for the recipient.

Maintaining a polite and professional tone is equally important. Avoid emotionally charged language, slang, or anything that could be perceived as aggressive or dismissive. Even when addressing disagreements or sensitive topics, remain courteous. Simple phrases like "Please" and "Thank you" go a long way in conveying professionalism and appreciation. Your written communication reflects your character, so ensure your tone remains respectful.

Formatting also plays a role in professionalism. Use standard, easy-to-read fonts like Times New Roman, Arial, or Calibri in point size 10, 11, or 12. Maintain consistent spacing and avoid excessive use of bold, italics, or underlining, which can make an email appear cluttered. A professional email signature that includes your name, title, contact information, and possibly your company logo adds credibility and ensures recipients can easily reach you.[18]

Managing attachments properly is another key aspect of email etiquette. File names should be clear and descriptive. Avoid generic names like "Document 1" or "File 1". Instead, use specific titles like "Project Proposal Final.docx" or "Client Report Q2 2025.pdf". If an attachment is large, consider compressing it to reduce the file size. Additionally, mention attachments in the body of the email to ensure the recipient knows they're included.

Timely responses are crucial for maintaining professional relationships and demonstrating reliability. Aim to reply within one business day or within a timeframe appropriate to the context. If a response requires more time, a brief acknowledgment email indicating when you'll provide a full reply is a considerate gesture. When replying, quote relevant portions of the original message to maintain clarity and context.

Beyond individual emails, managing your inbox effectively is essential for efficiency. Keep it organized by deleting unnecessary emails and categorizing important messages into folders. A well-maintained inbox makes it easier to locate specific conversations and respond promptly. Neglecting your email can create delays and give the impression of disorganization or inattention.

The "Reply All" function should be used with discretion. Overusing it can flood inboxes and frustrate recipients who don't need to be included in the conversation. Ensure that everyone on the recipient list genuinely needs the information before selecting this option. Similarly, while emojis and informal elements have become more common in digital communication, they should generally be avoided in professional emails to maintain a polished tone.

Tone is another crucial factor, especially since emails lack the vocal inflections and facial expressions that help convey intent in face-to-face conversations. Sarcasm, for example, can easily be misinterpreted. Before sending an email, you should consider reading it aloud to ensure your tone is clear and professional. If in doubt, a second pair of eyes can help catch potential misinterpretations and refine your message.

In an increasingly digital world, professional email etiquette remains a fundamental aspect of effective communication. By adhering to these guidelines, you project professionalism, respect, and a commitment to clear and efficient correspondence, qualities essential for success in any industry. Your email is often your first impression. Make it count. Investing time in crafting thoughtful, well-structured, and properly formatted emails strengthens your professional image and fosters better relationships with colleagues, clients, and stakeholders.

Engaging Respectfully and Appropriately

The widespread influence of social media in modern life demands a thoughtful approach to digital etiquette. While platforms like Twitter, Instagram, and Facebook may feel more casual than professional settings, the reality is that everything you post contributes to your online identity. A single careless comment or inappropriate post can have lasting personal and professional consequences. Given how quickly information spreads online, even minor lapses in judgment can escalate into significant issues. Developing a mindful, respectful, and strategic approach to social media is essential.

One of the key principles of social media etiquette is knowing your audience. Before posting, ask yourself: Who will see this? How might it be interpreted? A comment that may seem harmless among friends could be entirely inappropriate in a professional setting. Different platforms also call for different levels of formality. LinkedIn, for instance, demands a more polished and professional tone, while Instagram allows for more creative and personal expression. Being mindful of these distinctions helps you navigate social media effectively and ensures your content aligns with the expectations of each platform.

Your tone and language play a crucial role in how your message is received. While brevity is often appreciated in online communication, avoid being overly curt or dismissive. Sarcasm, which can be easily misinterpreted in text, should be avoided. Emojis and abbreviations can help convey emotion in casual conversations, but they may not always be appropriate in professional contexts. Strive for clarity and precision in your writing, ensuring that your message is easy to understand and free of ambiguity. Unlike face-to-face conversations, where tone and body language provide additional context, written communication relies solely on words. This makes it even more important to be clear, thoughtful, and intentional with your messaging.

Respectful engagement extends beyond your own posts since it includes how you interact with others. Respond to comments and messages in a timely manner, engage in meaningful discussions, and acknowledge different perspectives. However, avoid getting drawn into online arguments. If you disagree with someone, express your views respectfully and avoid personal attacks. The way you handle digital disagreements reflects your emotional intelligence and character. Even in moments of disagreement, maintaining a professional and composed demeanor strengthens your credibility.

Privacy is a critical aspect of social media etiquette. Be mindful of what you share, both about yourself and others. Avoid posting sensitive personal information, and regularly review your privacy settings to control who can access your content. Think twice before sharing photos or videos that could compromise your reputation or that of others. Once something is posted online, retracting it can be difficult, if not impossible. A moment of thoughtlessness today could have long-term consequences in the future.

Professional platforms like LinkedIn require an extra level of care. Your profile should be an accurate reflection of your skills, experience, and professional achievements. Avoid exaggerating or misrepresenting your credentials. When connecting with new contacts, personalize your requests to build genuine relationships rather than simply expanding your network for the sake of numbers. Participate in industry discussions by sharing insights and engaging respectfully with others' viewpoints. Since many employers and clients review online profiles before making decisions, maintaining a polished and professional presence on networking sites is essential for career growth.

Beyond professional platforms, your overall social media activity contributes to your personal brand. Even seemingly casual or humorous posts can shape how you're perceived by colleagues, clients, or potential employers. Employers often check candidates' social media profiles during the hiring process, and an inconsistent or unprofessional online presence can work against you. Strive to ensure that your social media activity aligns with the values and image you wish to project.

The visual aspect of your social media presence also matters. The quality of your profile photos, cover images, and shared media influences how you are perceived. A cluttered or inconsistent aesthetic may suggest a lack of attention to detail, whereas a well-organized, visually appealing profile signals professionalism and credibility. While every platform doesn't require a high level of polish, maintaining a clean and intentional digital presence enhances your online reputation.

While social media offers numerous opportunities, excessive use can lead to digital fatigue. Setting boundaries and limiting screen time allows for a healthier balance between your online and offline life. Taking regular breaks from social media can improve productivity, mental well-being, and overall perspective. A mindful approach to digital engagement not only prevents burnout but also fosters more meaningful and intentional interactions.

Mastering social media etiquette goes beyond following a set of rules. It's about being conscious and intentional in how you present yourself online. By engaging thoughtfully, respecting privacy, and maintaining professionalism, you can use social media to build meaningful connections and enhance your personal and professional reputation. Your online presence is a reflection of your values, character, and aspirations. It leaves a lasting impression, even in the fast-paced digital world. By fostering a responsible, respectful, and well-managed online identity, you ensure that your digital legacy aligns with your long-term goals. The principles of etiquette, refined over centuries, remain just as relevant in the digital age, guiding us toward respectful, thoughtful, and impactful interactions across all platforms.

CHAPTER 8

Protecting your Digital Footprint

The seamless integration of technology into our lives has undeniably revolutionized communication and access to information. However, this digital interconnectedness presents a new set of challenges, demanding a keen awareness of cybersecurity and privacy. Protecting your digital footprint is no longer optional. It's a necessity for maintaining your personal and professional integrity in the modern world. The careless sharing of information or the lack of robust security measures can lead to significant consequences, ranging from minor inconveniences to severe financial and reputational damage.

The first line of defense in safeguarding your digital presence is password management. Gone are the days when a simple password, easily guessed or cracked, sufficed. In today's sophisticated cyber landscape, employing robust and unique passwords for each online account is paramount. Consider utilizing a password manager, which is software that generates, stores, and manages complex passwords for you. These tools significantly reduce the risk of reusing passwords and falling victim to common password-cracking techniques. Beyond the strength of your passwords, the practice of regularly updating them is crucial. Frequent password changes, coupled with the use of multi-factor authentication, whenever possible, create a significant barrier against unauthorized access. Multi-factor authentication adds an extra layer of security, often requiring a code sent to your phone or email in addition to your password, making it exponentially harder for hackers to gain access.

Beyond passwords, securing your devices is equally critical. This includes keeping your operating systems, software, and apps updated with the latest security patches. Regular updates often contain critical security fixes that address vulnerabilities exploited by cybercriminals. Furthermore, installing reputable antivirus and anti-malware software is essential for detecting and neutralizing threats. These programs act as vigilant guardians, scanning your system for malicious code and preventing infections. Even seemingly innocuous emails or attachments can carry harmful viruses, so exercising caution and avoiding suspicious links is crucial.

The proliferation of phishing scams highlights the importance of critical thinking and skepticism in the digital realm. Phishing attempts often mimic legitimate communications from banks, institutions, or businesses, attempting to trick individuals into revealing sensitive information such as usernames, passwords, or credit card details.[19] Always verify the authenticity of any email or message requesting such information by contacting the organization directly through official channels. Never click on links or open attachments from unknown or suspicious sources.

Protecting personal information online extends beyond securing devices and passwords. It also involves being mindful of the data shared online. Before posting anything on social media, consider the potential implications. Oversharing personal details, such as your home address, birthday, or travel plans, can expose you to unnecessary risks. This information can be exploited by malicious actors for identity theft, stalking, or even physical harm. Similarly, be cautious about the information provided to websites and applications. Only share necessary information and always review privacy policies before agreeing to their terms of service. Understanding how data will be collected, used, and protected is crucial for maintaining control over your digital footprint.

The importance of privacy extends to online interactions. Be wary of sharing sensitive information in public forums or social media posts. Information shared online often persists indefinitely, meaning that even seemingly casual remarks can have lasting consequences. Consider the potential impact of your words before posting comments or engaging in online discussions. Maintaining a respectful and professional tone is not merely a matter of etiquette; it's a crucial element of protecting your online reputation.

In addition to personal data, protecting intellectual property is essential.

CHAPTER 8

If you create digital content, whether it be writing, images, or videos, take steps to safeguard your copyright. This might include watermarking work or registering copyrights with the appropriate authorities. Being proactive in protecting creative work can prevent unauthorized use and potential infringement.

The digital landscape is constantly evolving with new threats and challenges emerging regularly. Staying informed about the latest cybersecurity best practices is essential for maintaining digital security. Following cybersecurity news, attending webinars, and reading reputable sources can help individuals stay ahead of potential threats and adopt effective strategies for protecting their digital footprint.

Privacy settings on social media platforms offer a degree of control over who can access information. Familiarizing yourself with the privacy settings available on the platforms you use and configuring them to suit your comfort level is an important step in managing online security. Regularly reviewing and updating these settings ensures they remain aligned with privacy preferences. Carefully considering the level of detail shared in profiles and the extent to which others are allowed to interact with content can prevent unintended exposure of personal information.

Beyond personal vigilance, employing additional layers of security can further protect a digital presence. "A virtual private network, otherwise known as a VPN, encrypts an internet connection, making it more difficult for others to intercept online activity. This is particularly useful when using public Wi-Fi networks, which are often less secure[20]" than home or office networks. Regularly backing up data to an external hard drive or cloud storage service is another important precaution. This safeguard ensures that valuable information is not lost in the event of device failure or cyberattack.

In the digital age, reputation management is paramount. An online presence can significantly impact personal and professional life. Cultivating a positive and responsible online reputation requires mindful engagement and proactive measures to protect a digital footprint. Online actions have consequences, and maintaining a responsible digital presence is key to establishing and preserving a strong reputation.

The issue of data breaches is a growing concern in today's world. Large organizations and even smaller businesses are frequently targeted, leading to the exposure of vast amounts of personal information. Staying vigilant and understanding one's rights concerning data breaches is important. Understanding the procedures for reporting breaches and taking necessary steps to protect compromised information may mitigate potential damage.

Finally, the principles of etiquette extend into the digital realm. Just as politeness and respect are expected in face-to-face interactions, the same should be practiced online. Treating others with courtesy and respect, even when engaging in discussions on contentious topics, contributes to a more positive and constructive digital environment. The digital world, while offering vast opportunities for connection and communication, also demands a responsible and ethical approach to information sharing and online interactions. A digital footprint is a reflection of character and values, ensuring that it reflects the best version of oneself is essential.

Modern Etiquette in the Digital Age

The Golden Rule Reimagined for the Digital Age

The essence of civility remains unaltered in an era where interactions occur across screens rather than in drawing rooms. The rule that previously governed in-person conduct is now applicable to digital interactions as well: refrain from saying or doing anything that you would not say or do in person. This principle is not antiquated or quaint; rather, it's indispensable for the preservation of dignity in a digital world that is becoming more enduring and public.

A gentleman comprehends that his digital conduct is not exempt from the standards he maintains in person. Each comment, message, post, or reaction contributes to a more comprehensive narrative regarding his character. Grace, discretion, and restraint remain the fundamental principles of gentlemanly behavior, despite the evolution of technology. The objective should be consistent, regardless of whether one is responding to a direct message, composing a professional email, or engaging in a lively discussion on social media: to express oneself with integrity and decorum.

Common Mistakes in the Digital Era

New opportunities for connection have been introduced by digital communication, but it has also created new avenues for missteps. The subsequent are a few of the more prevalent errors that impair both perception and presence.

Passive Aggression and Subtweeting

Subtweeting is the act of posting a veiled or indirect criticism on social media, frequently directed at a specific individual without mentioning their identity. Although it may appear to be a cunning method of releasing frustration, it rarely leads to any productive results. Rather, it fosters an environment of suspicion and uncertainty, allowing others to engage in idle speculation and rumor.

A gentleman does not resort to public insinuations or coded barbs. It's advisable to address a matter in a private and direct manner if it necessitates discussion. If it does not, it's frequently more prudent to remain silent. Addressing grievances with clarity and discretion is indicative of maturity and guarantees that dignity is preserved.

Ghosting in Professional Environments

To "ghost" an individual is to abruptly cease all communication without providing an explanation. Although this term was first used in the context of dating, it has become more prevalent in the professional world. Examples of this include partnerships that are disregarded, collaborations that remain unresolved, and interviews that are not followed up on.

This conduct speaks volumes, and it's not in favor. A gentleman respects the time and effort of others. A brief and courteous note expressing appreciation and finality is the mark of true professionalism if he is no longer interested in pursuing an opportunity or is unable to respond in detail. Even when declining, it's possible to demonstrate respect.

Oversharing on Personal and Professional Platforms

The line between public and private has become increasingly ambiguous. Although a digital presence can be humanized by a certain degree of personal insight, oversharing can diminish mystique, weaken credibility, and appear emotionally indulgent.

A gentleman is as meticulous in his digital life as he is in his wardrobe. When conducted with dignity, sharing moments of accomplishment, contemplation, or gratitude is encouraged. Nevertheless, the audience is often subjected to emotional labor and scrutiny when grievances are expressed, personal drama is detailed, or excessive self-disclosure is engaged. It's advisable to inquire whether this serves a purpose, reflects favorably on oneself, or enhances the experience of another individual prior to posting.

CHAPTER 8

Lengthy Audio Messages or Unsolicited Voice Notes

Voice notes have become a prevalent mode of communication as a result of the proliferation of messaging applications. However, they are not universally embraced, particularly when they are sent without any prior notification or context. They necessitate a degree of attentiveness, privacy, and time that may not always be accessible.

Imagine receiving a three-minute voice message during a hectic weekday that lacks any indication of urgency. It necessitates dedication and disrupts concentration. The convenience of his correspondent is a factor that a gentleman takes into account. If a message is most effectively conveyed through voice, he either obtains permission or provides a written explanation before delivering it. As always, succinctness is a virtue.

Digital Character as Digital Presence

Your digital footprint is not merely a collection of posts and interactions; it's a silent reflection of your self-awareness, temperament, and values. In numerous instances, it will be encountered prior to your business card, voice, or salutation. Perception is significantly influenced by what remains online, whether intentionally or unintentionally.

A gentleman approaches his online presence with the same level of discipline, foresight, and consideration as he would his public behavior. He does not cultivate a persona that is disassociated from his authentic self, nor does he indulge in performative morality. Rather, he employs his digital presence to convey authenticity, not vanity; to connect, not to control; to share, not to show off.

The digital age has provided us with numerous advantages; however, it has also imposed upon us the obligation to maintain the highest standards of decorum and courtesy. Modern gentlemen comprehend that their online actions are as transparent as their in-person actions. He is grounded in a quiet confidence and unwavering reverence for others, regardless of whether it's in the form of emails, posts, messages, or even moments of silence. In doing so, he not only garners admiration but also commands attention.

Chapter 9

Building Meaningful Relationships – Connection and Legacy

Cultivating Meaningful Bonds

Friendship is the bedrock of a fulfilling life, a cornerstone often overlooked amidst the pursuit of professional success and material achievements. Cultivating meaningful friendships requires intentionality, effort, and a genuine commitment to nurturing these vital connections. It's about more than casual acquaintances; it's about forging bonds that provide support, encouragement, and shared experiences that enrich our lives.

At the heart of any enduring friendship is mutual respect. This means valuing the other person's opinions, even when they differ from your own. It involves active listening, showing empathy, and offering support without judgment. Respect also extends to understanding boundaries, honoring each other's time, and recognizing each individual's unique identity. A true friend celebrates your triumphs, provides comfort during hardships, and acknowledges the distinct path each person travels.

Open and honest communication is essential. Sharing your thoughts and feelings, both positive and negative, fosters trust and intimacy. Being vulnerable and authentic in your interactions deepens the connection. Transparent communication also allows for resolving conflicts before they escalate, ensuring that misunderstandings do not become lasting divisions. The goal is not to agree on everything but to engage in respectful dialogue and collaborate through disagreements.

Loyalty distinguishes genuine friendships from fleeting connections. A loyal friend stands by you through life's ebbs and flows, offering consistent support and encouragement. This loyalty is grounded in shared experiences and a profound understanding of each other's values. It involves being present during difficult times, providing honest feedback when necessary, and celebrating each other's successes wholeheartedly. True loyalty is not blind; it's an unwavering commitment rooted in mutual trust and care.

Shared experiences are the glue that binds friendships. Participating in activities you both enjoy, whether playing sports, pursuing hobbies, or traveling together, creates lasting memories and strengthens your bond. Spontaneous moments, such as late-night conversations or acts of kindness, add depth and richness to these relationships. These shared experiences foster a sense of camaraderie that transcends surface-level interactions.

Investing time and effort is crucial for maintaining friendships. Life's demands can be overwhelming, but making time for your friends demonstrates your commitment. Regular check-ins, spontaneous meetings, or planned gatherings keep the connection alive. Reflect on the frequency and quality of your interactions. Are you actively participating in each other's lives, or has the relationship become stagnant? Consistent engagement sustains the vitality of a friendship.

Balancing support and space is a delicate but essential aspect of friendship. There are times when a friend needs practical assistance or emotional support, and other times when they require solitude to process personal challenges. Being attuned to these needs, offering help when appropriate, and respecting their privacy fortifies a healthy relationship. Learning to navigate these dynamics with sensitivity deepens your ability to provide meaningful support.

Building new friendships, particularly in adulthood, may seem challenging but is deeply rewarding. Seek opportunities to meet new people through shared interests, community events, or professional networks. Be open to forming connections with individuals from diverse backgrounds. These new relationships can offer fresh perspectives and enrich your life in unexpected ways.

Maintaining long-distance friendships demands conscious effort. While physical proximity simplifies connection, distance does not preclude a meaningful relationship. Regular communication via calls, video chats, or messaging is vital. Making an effort to visit each other, when possible, reinforces the bond. Leveraging technology to stay connected ensures that even miles apart, you remain an integral part of each other's lives.

Conflict is inevitable in any relationship, including friendships. Addressing disagreements with patience and understanding is essential for preserving the relationship. Approach conflicts by listening to your friend's perspective, expressing your feelings calmly, and seeking a collaborative resolution. Avoid blame or personal attacks; instead, focus on the specific issue and work toward a solution that honors both viewpoints. Remember, the objective is not to "win" but to maintain and strengthen the bond.

Friendship is a journey that requires ongoing care and dedication. It evolves alongside life's changes and demands continuous nurturing. It's a reciprocal relationship requiring effort, patience, and mutual investment. By embracing key principles, including respect, communication, loyalty, shared experiences, time investment, supportive actions, and constructive conflict resolution, you cultivate friendships that stand the test of time.

The effort to foster and maintain genuine friendships is profoundly worthwhile. These relationships provide emotional support, joy, and a sense of belonging. They enrich your life in ways that material success cannot. In the end, the depth and quality of the friendships you cultivate reflect not only your character but also your commitment to living a meaningful and connected life.

Communication and Respect

Romantic relationships, unlike friendships, often involve a deeper level of emotional intimacy and commitment. While the principles of respect and communication remain paramount, the nuances within romance require a more delicate understanding. At the heart of any successful romantic relationship are two pillars: open and honest communication, and unwavering mutual respect. Without these, the relationship is built on shifting sands, vulnerable to the inevitable storms of life.

"Effective communication is more than just talking; it's truly listening and understanding your partner's perspective.[21]" This involves active listening; not just hearing the words, but paying attention to tone, body language, and the unspoken emotions behind them.[22] Often, what remains unsaid speaks volumes. Learning to interpret these subtle cues is crucial for understanding your partner's needs and concerns. Creating a safe space where both partners feel comfortable expressing their thoughts and feelings without fear of judgment fosters emotional intimacy and trust.

"When communicating, it's essential to avoid accusatory language. Instead use 'I' statements to express feelings without placing blame.[23] For instance, rather than saying, "You always leave the dishes dirty", try, "I feel frustrated when the dishes are left undone, as it adds to my workload". This small shift in phrasing can transform the tone of a conversation, making it more collaborative rather than confrontational. Beyond words, nonverbal cues play a significant role. Maintaining eye contact, offering gentle touches, and being physically present demonstrate attentiveness and affection. Conversely, dismissive body language or constant distractions, like checking your phone, signal disinterest and disrespect.

Respect in a romantic relationship is not simply the absence of conflict; it's an active demonstration of valuing your partner's thoughts, feelings, and boundaries. This includes recognizing their independence, supporting their personal growth, and avoiding controlling or manipulative behaviors. A healthy relationship empowers both individuals to pursue their own goals while sharing a common life together. Respect also means embracing differences without attempting to change your partner. Constructive conflict resolution is key through focusing on understanding each other rather than "winning" the argument.

Part of showing respect involves acknowledging and accepting your partner's past. Making disparaging remarks about their previous relationships can foster insecurity and distrust. Instead, focus on building a future together and celebrating your shared journey. Additionally, maintaining personal space is crucial. While spending quality time together strengthens intimacy, it's equally important to allow your partner the freedom to pursue their interests and friendships.[24] This balance between closeness and autonomy fosters a sustainable and respectful relationship.

Understanding and supporting your partner's values and aspirations is another vital aspect of respect. This means engaging in open conversations, showing empathy, and adapting to their evolving goals. Whether it involves career ambitions or personal growth, offering encouragement and celebrating their achievements reinforces your commitment. Mutual support, especially during challenging times, strengthens the emotional foundation of the relationship.

In today's digital age, respecting your partner also extends to online behavior. Responsible social media habits, such as avoiding public conflicts and maintaining privacy, demonstrate thoughtfulness and care. Clear digital boundaries are as essential as physical ones in fostering a healthy partnership. Treating your relationship with the same discretion you would afford your most cherished possessions reflects a deep sense of respect and commitment.

Maintaining a romantic relationship requires continuous effort, adaptability, and mutual investment. Relationships are dynamic; they evolve as individuals grow and circumstances change. Regular reflection on the relationship's dynamics and open discussions about individual needs are essential for sustaining long-term success. This involves navigating the balance between personal autonomy and shared commitments while fostering an environment of emotional safety and trust.

Intimacy, both physical and emotional, requires conscious effort. Regularly dedicating time to connect, whether through shared activities or meaningful conversations, nurtures the bond between partners. While physical intimacy is important, a truly fulfilling relationship is built on a foundation of emotional connection and mutual support. Prioritizing quality time, fostering open dialogue, and offering unwavering emotional support are critical for maintaining a strong, intimate bond. Seeking external help when needed is not a sign of weakness but a testament to the relationship's importance.

Couples counseling provides a neutral space for addressing challenges and developing effective communication strategies. Proactively seeking professional guidance demonstrates a mature commitment to nurturing and preserving the relationship. Just as we seek expert advice in other areas of life, investing in the health of our relationships reflects a dedication to their longevity and well-being.

Ultimately, a successful romantic relationship is not just a partnership, but it's a shared journey of growth, support, and mutual respect. This journey requires continuous effort, a willingness to navigate challenges together, and an ongoing commitment to understanding and valuing each other. By fostering open communication, demonstrating respect, and prioritizing emotional connection, couples can build a lasting bond that weathers life's inevitable changes and deepens over time.

Nurturing Bonds across Generations

Family relationships form the bedrock of our lives, shaping our identities and providing a profound sense of belonging. Unlike friendships or romantic partnerships, which are often chosen, familial ties are inherently interwoven into our existence. These relationships carry both a unique weight of responsibility and an extraordinary opportunity for growth and connection. Nurturing intergenerational bonds requires conscious effort, understanding, and a willingness to adapt to the ever-changing dynamics within the family unit. This is even more essential in today's fast-paced world, where geographical distances and differing lifestyles can strain even the strongest connections.

The Power of Open and Honest Communication

At the heart of strong family relationships lies open and honest communication. This goes beyond polite exchanges during holiday gatherings. It involves actively listening to and valuing the perspectives and experiences of each family member, regardless of age. Grandparents, for instance, offer a wealth of life experience that can provide invaluable guidance to younger generations. Their stories and insights ground the family in its history and heritage. Conversely, younger family members bring fresh perspectives and technological fluency that can enrich the lives of older relatives.

True communication demands active listening, being a conscious effort to understand beyond words. This means putting aside distractions, making eye contact, and demonstrating genuine interest. Thoughtful questions can deepen the connection. Instead of a generic "How are you doing?", asking, "What's been the highlight of your week?" or "Is there something I can do to support you?" fosters meaningful dialogue and a stronger emotional bond.

Consistent Engagement: Small Gestures Matter

Maintaining family ties does not require daily contact but thrives on consistent, intentional engagement. Regular phone calls, video chats, emails, and even handwritten letters serve as reminders of enduring love and support. Sharing photos or simply sending a brief "thinking of you" message can significantly strengthen these connections. Consistency is key because frequent, small gestures often have a more lasting impact than infrequent grand displays.

Family traditions also play a pivotal role in nurturing intergenerational bonds. Shared experiences, whether large celebrations or simple activities like baking together or watching a favorite movie, create lasting memories and reinforce collective identity. Creating new traditions, especially ones involving multiple generations, can further strengthen connections. For example, maintaining a family journal where members contribute thoughts and reflections fosters a shared narrative and deepens familial ties.

Embracing Generational Differences

Every generation is shaped by its own unique experiences, values, and societal influences. These differences can lead to misunderstandings, but when approached with curiosity and respect, they become opportunities for learning and growth. Rather than focusing on disagreements, families can find common ground by identifying shared values and activities that bridge generational gaps.

Understanding and respecting generational differences also requires acknowledging the evolving roles within the family. Younger members can offer practical assistance and emotional support to older relatives, while elders can provide wisdom and perspective. Recognizing and valuing each family member's contributions fosters an environment of mutual respect and appreciation.

Addressing and Healing Family Conflicts

Unresolved conflicts and past hurts can fracture family relationships if left unaddressed. Healing requires humility, empathy, and a willingness to forgive. While not all conflicts necessitate formal confrontation, small gestures of understanding or heartfelt conversations can facilitate reconciliation. In some cases, professional support through family therapy provides a safe space for open dialogue and healing.

The willingness to seek professional help is a testament to a family's commitment to strengthening bonds. Just as we seek expert guidance in other aspects of life, turning to a family counselor demonstrates a proactive approach to preserving and enhancing familial relationships.

Providing Practical and Emotional Support

Supporting family members involves both emotional care and practical assistance. For elderly relatives, this may mean helping with household tasks, arranging medical appointments, or simply offering companionship. Younger family members may benefit from career guidance, emotional support, or financial advice. Tailoring support to each individual's unique needs reinforces their sense of value and belonging.

Being present for significant milestones, including birthdays, graduations, weddings, and actively participating in everyday moments signals that each family member is cherished. In our fast-paced world, making time for these meaningful moments is a powerful expression of love and commitment.

Adapting to Change and Embracing Growth

Family relationships are dynamic and evolve over time. As members grow and life circumstances change, flexibility and adaptability become essential. This includes welcoming new family members, adjusting to shifting roles, and navigating life transitions. Acknowledging that family is a living, evolving entity helps sustain strong bonds over time.

By investing in family relationships through consistent communication, meaningful engagement, and mutual respect, we cultivate a legacy of love and support that transcends generations. These efforts enrich our own lives while laying the foundation for future family members to experience the same enduring sense of connection and belonging. In nurturing these bonds, we create not just a family, but a lasting legacy of love and unity.

Guiding and Supporting Others

Mentorship goes beyond simply offering advice; it's a meaningful exchange of experience, wisdom, and support, fostering growth in both the mentor and mentee. It's a reciprocal relationship, a balance between seasoned expertise and eager ambition. In today's fast-paced world, where information is abundant but genuine guidance is rare, the role of a mentor is increasingly vital. This isn't just about career advancement; it's about navigating life's complexities with greater confidence and understanding.

The benefits of mentorship stretch far beyond the professional realm. A mentor provides valuable insights into personal growth, helping you identify your strengths, overcome weaknesses, and build greater self-awareness. This guidance proves invaluable during life's transitions, from career changes to personal challenges, offering a safe space for exploration and self-discovery. The relationship fosters resilience; setbacks become less intimidating with a trusted advisor to offer perspective and support.

CHAPTER 9

Finding the right mentor requires careful thought and proactive engagement. It's not just about selecting someone successful in your field; it's about choosing someone whose values align with yours, someone whose qualities you admire and wish to emulate. Look for individuals who display integrity, empathy, and a sincere commitment to your growth. Networking events, professional organizations, and your own circles are great places to find potential mentors. Don't hesitate to approach those you respect because often a thoughtful, well-crafted request opens doors to unexpected opportunities.

Once the mentor-mentee relationship is established, it requires nurturing and respect. Regular communication is key, whether through formal meetings, informal chats, or even emails. Be punctual and prepared for meetings, showing your commitment to the relationship. Actively listen to your mentor's advice, ask insightful questions, and be eager to learn. Remember, mentorship is a collaborative process; while your mentor provides guidance, your growth depends on your efforts and dedication. Consider keeping a journal to track insights, challenges, and action points from your mentoring sessions. This will serve as a tangible record of your progress and offer reference points for future conversations.

The success of a mentorship extends beyond exchanging advice. It's about building a relationship based on mutual respect, trust, and open communication. This means being honest about your challenges and goals, even when they feel uncomfortable to share. A strong mentor-mentee relationship provides a safe space for vulnerability, enabling you to explore your doubts and insecurities without fear of judgment. This openness fosters a deeper connection and leads to more meaningful guidance. Don't forget to show gratitude for your mentor's time and support, and acknowledge their commitment to your growth.

On the flip side, mentoring is equally fulfilling and demanding. It requires a genuine desire to help, patience, and a willingness to share knowledge and experience. Effective mentorship involves listening actively, providing constructive criticism, and offering unwavering support. It's about guiding not directing; empowering not controlling. A good mentor serves as a sounding board, offering fresh perspectives and challenging assumptions. They help mentees identify blind spots and develop strategies to overcome obstacles. Mentorship should be approached with humility, recognizing that everyone has unique strengths and challenges.

An effective mentor tailors their guidance to the specific needs and goals of their mentee. This means taking the time to understand their aspirations, challenges, and learning style. It requires empathy and the flexibility to adjust your approach based on how the mentee responds. This personalized method ensures the mentoring relationship is both effective and rewarding for both parties. Furthermore, a good mentor encourages independence, aiming not to create dependency but to equip the mentee with the skills and confidence needed to face challenges on their own.

Beyond the immediate benefits for both mentor and mentee, mentorship fosters a broader sense of community and professional growth. It cultivates a culture of collaboration and knowledge-sharing, strengthening organizations and industries. Companies that promote mentorship programs often see higher employee engagement, retention, and productivity. Mentorship is an investment in future leadership, shaping the next generation of professionals and influencing the future of their fields. By building a culture of mentorship, organizations lay the groundwork for sustainable growth and innovation.

Becoming a mentor is not a passive process; it demands active involvement and a commitment to personal and professional development. Mentors must continuously reflect on their experiences, seek new insights, and stay current in their field. They should engage in professional development, consistently honing their mentoring skills. This ongoing growth benefits the mentor while ensuring they can provide relevant and effective guidance.

CHAPTER 9

Mentorship, then, is not merely an exchange of knowledge because it becomes a long-term relationship grounded in mutual respect, trust, and shared growth. The benefits stretch far beyond the immediate context, shaping careers, lives, and fostering a sense of community that transcends individual ambitions. It highlights the enduring power of human connection and the impact of shared experiences. By embracing effective mentorship principles, both mentors and mentees unlock their potential, leaving a lasting legacy across generations. Mentorship is a journey of shared growth, a testament to human connection, and a contribution to a more supportive world. It's an investment in both personal and collective futures, cultivating a culture of growth, empowerment, and shared success. This dynamic doesn't just advance individuals; it creates a ripple effect of positive influence that extends far beyond the mentor-mentee relationship.

The modern gentleman understands mentorship's reciprocal nature. He sees the opportunity not only to receive guidance but also to share his experience and wisdom with others. This approach strengthens the community, promoting a culture of collaboration and mutual support. It also enhances personal growth, as mentoring deepens self-awareness and hones leadership skills. A gentleman's legacy extends beyond his personal achievements; it includes the lives he has touched and the positive impact he has had on the world. Mentorship plays a crucial role in shaping that legacy, leaving a lasting mark on future generations. It's a powerful demonstration of leadership, a selfless act of guidance, and an investment in the collective good. Mentoring isn't just about passing on knowledge; it's about nurturing potential, fostering resilience, and empowering others to reach their fullest potential. This contributes to a stronger, more vibrant community, reflecting the qualities of a refined gentleman. The responsibility doesn't solely rest with the mentor; the mentee also plays a key role in ensuring the success and longevity of the relationship. Active self-reflection, seeking feedback, and applying the lessons learned are essential for continuous growth.

The impact of a successful mentorship reaches far beyond the individual. It influences networks, industries, and shapes society as a whole. Empowered individuals contribute more effectively to their communities, businesses, and society. Mentorship nurtures a culture of learning, adaptability, and innovation; a catalyst for social progress that highlights our interconnectedness. Cultivating effective mentorship is not just a personal endeavor but a societal responsibility. Embracing this responsibility reflects the essence of the modern gentleman, one who seeks not only personal growth but the betterment of the world around him. His legacy isn't in material possessions but in the lives that he has touched, the potential he's unlocked, and the lasting positive impact he's made. Mentorship isn't just a valuable skill but it's a moral imperative for those pursuing a life of purpose and lasting significance.

Contributing to Society

Leaving a lasting impact goes beyond accumulating wealth or professional recognition. It's about the ripple effect of one's actions, the positive influence on others' lives, and a meaningful contribution to the greater good. A gentleman of substance understands this profound truth and actively seeks ways to make a difference in society. This isn't about grand gestures or lofty declarations but it's more about consistent, thoughtful actions that reflect a commitment to ethics, social responsibility, and the betterment of humanity.

One of the most effective ways to contribute to society is through active involvement in charitable endeavors. This isn't simply about writing a check; it's about deeply engaging with the cause, understanding its challenges, and investing time and energy. Consider volunteering at a local soup kitchen, mentoring underprivileged youth, or supporting organizations focused on environmental conservation or medical research. Donating your time and skills is far more impactful than monetary contributions alone; it shows dedication to the cause, fosters authentic connections, and makes a tangible difference in the lives of those in need. Direct participation also provides a richer understanding of the issues faced by vulnerable communities, nurturing empathy and a sense of shared humanity.

CHAPTER 9

Contributing to society can take many forms beyond formal charitable work. Supporting local businesses, patronizing ethical companies, and advocating for responsible consumption are subtle yet powerful ways to spark positive change. A gentleman understands the interconnectedness of economic systems and recognizes his role in promoting a more equitable and environmentally conscious marketplace. This involves making informed decisions about where to spend, supporting businesses that uphold ethical labor practices and environmental sustainability, and actively discouraging harmful practices. The cumulative effect of these choices can be substantial, creating demand for responsible business practices and rewarding companies that prioritize ethical conduct.

Civic engagement is another fundamental responsibility. This includes staying informed about current events, participating in the democratic process, and advocating for policies that benefit the community and the nation. Voting, engaging in respectful political discourse, and participating in local initiatives are all essential parts of civic duty. A gentleman uses his voice thoughtfully, advocating for positive change and standing against injustice. His role as a responsible citizen is key to creating a more just and equitable society.

As discussed earlier, mentorship is also a powerful way to leave a lasting impact. By guiding and supporting younger generations, a gentleman helps develop future leaders, creating a legacy of knowledge, wisdom, and ethical conduct. This is a two-way street because mentorship enriches both mentor and mentee. The experience of sharing knowledge is deeply rewarding, and witnessing the growth and success of a mentee brings immense personal fulfillment. Moreover, the influence of effective mentorship spreads beyond the individual, creating a network of support and amplifying positive change across communities and industries.

Beyond formal mentorship, simply being a positive role model can leave a profound impact. By demonstrating integrity, kindness, and respect in everyday interactions, a gentleman positively influences those around him. Practicing empathy, active listening, and mindful communication helps foster a culture of kindness and mutual respect. These actions, while seemingly small, have a cumulative effect that creates a more compassionate social environment. Through consistent ethical behavior, a gentleman inspires others to adopt these qualities, enhancing the collective atmosphere of his community.

Building a strong sense of community is equally important. This involves participating in local organizations, forging meaningful connections with neighbors and colleagues, and contributing to the overall well-being of the community. Joining local clubs, attending community events, and volunteering for initiatives are just a few ways to create a sense of belonging and nurture a thriving community environment. Engaged citizens form the foundation of strong communities, and a gentleman plays a key role in fostering this type of environment.

Intellectual and artistic contributions also help leave a lasting legacy. Supporting the arts, engaging in intellectual pursuits, and encouraging creativity enrich the cultural landscape. This might involve attending concerts, theater performances, and art exhibitions, or simply engaging in thought-provoking conversations. Promoting intellectual curiosity and artistic expression strengthens a society's innovation, critical thinking, and appreciation for beauty. These contributions lead to a more fulfilling and dynamic life for all members of the community.

Finally, environmental stewardship is an essential element of leaving a lasting legacy. A gentleman recognizes the importance of preserving the planet for future generations and acts accordingly. This includes adopting eco-friendly practices in his personal life, supporting organizations focused on conservation, and advocating for policies that promote sustainability. Whether reducing his carbon footprint, backing renewable energy projects, or participating in environmental cleanups, he understands that collective

CHAPTER 9

action is key to mitigating climate change and preserving natural resources. These efforts ensure a vibrant planet for future generations.

Leaving a lasting impact is not a single act but an ongoing process of thoughtful engagement and dedication to making the world better. It requires self-reflection, ethical conduct, and a commitment to investing time and energy in positive change. A gentleman who embraces this mindset leaves a legacy beyond material possessions; he leaves a legacy of influence, integrity, and lasting contributions to the greater good. This legacy is the true measure of a life well-lived, more specifically a life committed to purpose and significance. It's built not on fleeting achievements but on the enduring impact of a life driven by compassion, integrity, and a dedication to improving the world.

References

[1] FasterCapital [Internet]. [cited 2025 Mar 23]. Vocal Tone. Available from: https://fastercapital.com/keyword/vocal-tone.html/1

[2] Men's Travel Fashion: How to Stay Stylish While on the Road [Internet]. Modern Gentleman. 2023 [cited 2025 Mar 23]. Available from: https://www.moderngentlemanmagazine.com/mens-travel-fashion-tips/

[3] 6 Steps to Gracefully End a First Date - Dating [Internet]. [cited 2025 Mar 24]. Available from: https://www.enotalone.com/article/dating/6-steps-to-gracefully-end-a-first-date-r12955/

[4] 5 ways to set boundaries with your live-in boyfriend [Internet]. 2024 [cited 2025 Mar 24]. Available from: https://rollingout.com/2024/08/30/5-ways-set-boundaries-live-in-boyfriend/

[5] 7 Surprising Body Language Secrets (You Must Know!) - Personal Growth [Internet]. [cited 2025 Mar 24]. Available from: https://www.enotalone.com/article/personal-growth/7-surprising-body-language-secrets-you-must-know-r14142/

[6] Character AI User Interactions: Redefining User Experiences [Internet]. [cited 2025 Mar 24]. Available from: https://aiforsocialgood.ca/blog/character-ai-user-interactions

[7] Remodelista [Internet]. 2013 [cited 2025 Mar 24]. Expert Advice: How to Set the Table, Courtesy of Food 52. Available from: https://www.remodelis

REFERENCES

ta.com/posts/expert-advice-setting-the-table-with-food-52/

[8] 10 Physician Etiquette Tips, Navigating a Formal Meal [Internet]. [cited 2025 Mar 24]. Available from: https://www.physicianspractice.com/view/10-physician-etiquette-tips-navigating-formal-meal

[9] Ibid

[10] Ibid

[11] Inc CM. Currency Mart Inc. [cited 2025 Mar 24]. What Is Bridal Shower. Available from: https://currencymart.net/answer-public-what/what-is-bridal-shower/index.html

[12] Ibid

[13] Navigating Cultural Intelligence In The UK For Indian Technologists [Internet]. [cited 2025 Mar 24]. Available from: https://www.forbes.com/councils/forbesbusinesscouncil/2024/02/08/tips-for-navigating-cultural-intelligence-in-the-uk-for-indian-technologists/

[14] Mastering the Art of Business Communication: A Key to Success | by Lahiru Wijewardhana | Medium [Internet]. [cited 2025 Mar 24]. Available from: https://medium.com/@aglwijewardhana/mastering-the-art-of-business-communication-a-key-to-success-cc53711e5e1b

[15] CAROLYN WATSON CONDUCTOR - Blog | Carolyn Watson Conductor [Internet]. [cited 2025 Mar 24]. Available from: https://carolyn-watson-conductor.weebly.com/blog

[16] Ibid

[17] FasterCapital [Internet]. [cited 2025 Mar 23]. Simple Language. Available

from: https://fastercapital.com/keyword/simple-language.html

[18] HUSS 360 - Lecture 5 - Written and Ongoing Communication.docx - HUSS360 - Lecture 5 - Written and Ongoing Communication Lesson # 1 -Social Media and | Course Hero [Internet]. [cited 2025 Mar 24]. Available from: https://www.coursehero.com/file/173323627/HUSS-360-Lecture-5-Written-and-Ongoing-Communicationdocx/

[19] FasterCapital [Internet]. [cited 2025 Mar 24]. Complex Passwords. Available from: https://fastercapital.com/keyword/complex-passwords.html

[20] SchoolsFirst FCU | Stay Safe Online: Six Tips to Protect Your Identity [Internet]. [cited 2025 Mar 24]. Available from: https://www.schoolsfirstfcu.org/advice/financial-wellness/fraud/stay-safe-online-5-tips-to-protect-your-identity/

[21] Communication Is Key to Any Healthy Relationship, But it's Not Always Easy to Do - The Good Men Project [Internet]. [cited 2025 Mar 24]. Available from: https://goodmenproject.com/featured-content/communication-is-key-to-any-healthy-relationship-but-its-not-always-easy-to-do/

[22] FasterCapital [Internet]. [cited 2025 Mar 23]. Meaningful Conversations. Available from: https://fastercapital.com/keyword/meaningful-conversations.html

[23] 5 ways to set boundaries with your live-in boyfriend [Internet]. 2024 [cited 2025 Mar 24]. Available from: https://rollingout.com/2024/08/30/5-ways-set-boundaries-live-in-boyfriend/

[24] 5 Secrets to Understanding What Women Want [Internet]. 2023 [cited 2025 Mar 24]. Available from: https://www.enotalone.com/article/relationships/5-secrets-to-understanding-what-women-want-r10265/

Acknowledgements

This book is the culmination of not only my own efforts but also the unwavering support, love, and guidance of the extraordinary people in my life.

To my partner, Brendan Balazs, thank you for your patience, encouragement, and belief in me throughout this journey. Your love and steadfast support were my anchor during the countless hours spent writing, editing, and refining these pages.

To my parents, Teresa Costa and Charlie Pavia, you have shaped me into the person I am today. Your example of hard work, professionalism, respect, and courtesy has been my foundation, and I carry your lessons with me in everything I do.

To my grandmothers, Fernanda and Maria, your wisdom and kindness left an indelible mark on my character. You taught me that true etiquette begins with thoughtfulness and a genuine consideration for others, which are values I aspire to uphold and share through this book.

To my dear friend Elly, thank you for challenging me to remain socially aware and for your invaluable insights into the ever-evolving world of fashion and etiquette. Your sharp eye and candid advice kept me on my toes and reminded me of the importance of always striving for excellence.

Each of you has contributed to this book in ways both big and small and, for that, I am eternally grateful. This work is as much a reflection of your influence as it's my own. Thank you for walking this journey with me.

Author Biography

Daniel Pavia is a seasoned etiquette enthusiast and style connoisseur with extensive experience navigating both corporate and social spheres. With over two decades of expertise in sales and leadership, Daniel has refined his skills in presentation, protocol, and personal branding, making him a natural authority in the art of modern etiquette.

Drawing inspiration from his background in strategic leadership and organizational management, Daniel's approach blends timeless sophistication with contemporary sensibilities. His career includes leading high-performing teams, training sales executives, and pioneering innovative strategies, all of which shape his ability to communicate the nuances of refinement and poise.

A passionate advocate for individuality and self-expression, Daniel focuses on empowering people to cultivate confidence, grace, and authenticity in all aspects of their lives. He believes that mastering etiquette isn't about adhering to rigid rules, but rather about embracing respect, understanding, and thoughtful consideration for others.

As the author of *The Gentleman's Dominion: A Foundational Guide to Professional and Social Etiquette*, Daniel shares practical insights on navigating social and professional settings with confidence. Outside of writing, he enjoys good conversation, a well-made drink, and the occasional opportunity to prove that manners and mischief aren't mutually exclusive.

www.ingramcontent.com/pod-product-compliance
Lightning Source LLC
LaVergne TN
LVHW072021060526
838200LV00009B/226